A

LOOK BACK WITH TEARS

LOOK BACK WITH TEARS

by

Joe Murphy

ALTRINCHAM

JOHN SHERRATT AND SON LTD

First published 1976
by John Sherratt and Son Ltd.,
78 Park Road, Altrincham

© Joe Murphy 1976

ISBN 0 85427 048 5

Made and printed in Great Britain

and bound by
John Sherratt and Son Ltd.,
Gloucester Street, Manchester

I dedicate this book to:

MY MOTHER, who worked and struggled for her family.

MY FATHER, who provided for us.

MY BROTHERS AND SISTERS, as a memento of our life together.

KATHLEEN, who as a girl, loved and waited for six years for my return from war, married me and blessed our union with two fine sons, who in turn, gave us two lovely daughters-in-law and four beautiful grandchildren.

We have at the time of writing this book, been married for thirty happy years.

It is my past that holds me, yet binds me to my future.

FOREWORD

This is a true story based on fact. Names and places are fictional in most cases, and bear no resemblance to anyone, living or dead. Owing to difficulty in comprehension by the uninitiated, the Derbyshire dialect has not been adhered to.

I have written this book in the hope that the reader will find enjoyment in its contents. For the older reader, a taste of nostalgia; for the younger, a look at life in the thirties.

It has been written from memory and not from kept records or diaries. Some of the events could be a little inaccurate, for which I apologize. Dates and places of battles have been purposely omitted in case it causes distress to anyone who could relate dates and places with a loved one. Only territories are thus named.

October 30th, 1919

Joe was born, the story is told,
No silver spoon, no hoard of gold.
No pram to lay; to sleep, a wooden cradle;
His lullaby, clatter of horses from the stable.
Clogs on feet, and trams that sway
On lines on cobbled street.

'Hard times for you', these words were said
To this infant, small and new.
Many's the tear you will shed,
No princely crown for your head,
No wise men, Kings from afar,
No guiding star,
No homage paid to this little lad,
Only brothers and sisters,
Mam and dad.

Chapter One

'ENVIRONMENT'

I was born after the First World War in the year 1919. This chapter follows my childhood and my path into manhood. It deals with my family and their way of life, their joys, their hopes and their fears, the environment they lived in.

My name is Joe. I was born the eighth child of a man just back from the war, who had been wounded and taken prisoner nine months before the war ended. He had suffered in mind and body and was a changed man. He seemed to lack emotion and he drank, maybe too much. He came from a good and respected family, was well educated and had a good job. Then the war came in 1914 and changed everything. He still worked hard at a job he was probably lucky to get, a labourer in a gas works. He provided for his family as best he could, against terrible odds and conditions that prevailed at the time. He always seemed to be working and drinking. Like my brothers, I was frightened of him. In fact, many a good hiding was given to one or the other, but for what?—who knows.

My Mam was a gentle little woman, dedicated to her family, a protector of her flock from the wrath of Dad when he came in drunk. Her life was one long drudge of work and worry, making her look older than her years. It was a daily struggle to keep body and soul together, and as she was a God-fearing woman, she made sure that the children went to church when they were old enough. That would look after their souls, she thought. But what of their bodies? She had to do that alone with any money she had saved from the housekeeping. Her visits round the shops were to find the food that was both

9

nourishing and cheap. Some of the better foods were out of reach of the little tattered purse she always carried whether it be empty or full (the latter very rare). She had to get the food that would help guard them against the diseases of the day—scarlet fever, diphtheria, etc., and the dreaded rickets that left children with bow-legs or knock-knees. The Spanish 'flu was at that time raging through Europe, taking many thousands of lives. With the little money that Dad provided, it made it very hard for Mam to maintain this vital nourishment so badly needed for growing children. The other big problem for Mam was clothing for their bodies. This meant weekly visits to the jumble sales held at the schools and halls around the town.

Religion was no barrier to Mam. Whether it be Baptist, Salvation Army or whatever, where there was a bargain, there was Mam. With the largest bags she could find and probably one or two of the older lads, she would set off, clutching her old tattered purse. The lads would feel ashamed, but not Mam. She would push and shove round the tables, looking for clogs, shoes, trousers, anything she thought might do for one or other of the children. It didn't even matter if things were a bit big; a penny for this, a penny for that—they were bargains.

Mam was a determined woman, ever since she lost her little twin girls. They died when they were three years old from pneumonia. She was determined not to lose any more. She had five now, and with my arrival it made six, and three more were to follow in the next few years.

The town I was born in nestled snuggly in a valley surrounded by the Pennine hills. The main source of employment was the cotton mills where most of the town's inhabitants seemed to work, judging by the sound of clogged feet clattering their way to the various mills with their tall chimneys belching out smoke, blotting out the sky. There was also a large paper mill on the outskirts of the town, and the cut logs destined for that mill could be heard being unloaded daily from the railway wagons into a large and spacious yard, the labour force being provided by the labour exchange. They would send the men down there just to stand in the hope of having their names called out, just to earn a few 'bob'. There would be fifty or sixty men in cloth caps.

'Wi may be lucky today, Jim,' someone would say.

'I bloody hope so, Jack. I've had nowt for weeks now,' would be the reply.

'I just want ten o' you today, that's all. I'll call yer names, then the rest of yer can bugger off,' the foreman called out. After he had got the men he wanted, the remainder would break up into small groups and wander aimlessly to their favourite street corner to stand and while away the time. Someone would have the racing paper and the usual talk that could be heard was:

'I fancy Gordon Richards' mount in three-thirty at Newmarket today. What's tha fancy?'

They talked as if they had plenty of money, while at the same time they would have two fingers in their waistcoat pocket feeling for tab ends.

'Hast a match, Jack?' one would say.

'Have this one,' he'd say, handing him a match he'd found loose in his pocket. The one who had asked would take it, strike it on the wall and nearly burn his nose trying to light the small end of the cigarette in his mouth. Then someone would most likely say,

'Give us a swallow before it's all gone.'

This sort of thing was a daily routine with a lot of these chaps. They wanted work, but that wasn't available. Just a few days on the logs if they were lucky and a bit of snow-shifting in the winter.

We had the gasworks practically in the centre of the town, a convenient place to build it, but very unsightly and smelly. My father's place of work, the big gasometer, stored the gas that gave light to the town's streets and houses. Lamp posts that looked like gallows stood on every cobbled street corner, giving off an eerie light so dim as the lamp-lighter man went round with a big hooked stick, lighting them. Children would congregate round these lamp posts like moths round a candle, to play, using their mam's clothes line to tie on to the lamp and swing round. They would swing round and round, shaking the lamp until finally the frail mantle broke. Then the children ran away, most likely to play at another one.

Rows and rows of cottage houses, the two-up-and-two-down type, housed the working class. It was unbelievable how so many could possibly live in these small dwellings, for most of them seemed to have large families. On every corner, like the lamp post, we had the 'pub'. These always seemed to be full, despite the scarcity of money. Women would look for their husbands and know that they were in one or other of these pubs. This happened more so on pay day at the 'dole'. They had to make sure they didn't spend what pittance they got. Many's the time a woman could be heard,

'If tha doesn't come out now, Jack Robinson, I'll come in and drag thee out.'

This usually did the trick. He would come out, for he didn't like being shown up.

The town seemed to be divided, not by design but by chance, the better-off on the top side and the working class on the lower side, the railway acting as the dividing line. The cotton mills, the cottages and the gasworks were on the lower side, this side of the track. At the top side, were the lovely semi-detached houses, the detached and palatial mansions, housing the very rich, with their butlers and maids and horse-drawn carriages; the mill owners and benefactors to the town, the ones who could afford to give something or other: a water trough for the horses or park benches with their names inscribed on a brass plate. Yes, they wanted the town to remember them.

The town had its beauty too. This was found in its parks and in its surrounding hills, seen in all their glory in the summer months; when the brass bands played in their decorated bandstands, when husband and wife could spend a restful hour while their children played on the swings or paddled in the brooks, when boy could meet girl and girl meet boy. What better setting could there be than this? In and out of the gardens they strolled as the bandsmen in bright and colourful uniforms played their lovely melodies; the flowers too, showing off in their full glory.

When not in the park, the more energetic would have a ramble over the hills surrounding the town, or if you owned a cycle then it was a ride. Either way, you would climb up and up until you thought you could touch the sky, breathe in and fill your lungs with clean, fresh air, something you couldn't get in the town. You could drink at the ever-flowing cool springs that dotted the landscape and sit amongst the heather and gaze in wonder at nature's splendour. Feeling so free from the bonds in the town beneath, you'd take a long piece of grass, put it in your mouth, place your hands behind your head and lay back and relax with your thoughts, with the sun's rays lulling you into tranquillity. The setting of the sun and the rumble in your tummy would tell you it was time to wend your way home.

After tea this Sunday and every Sunday, was the time to wash and brush up, to look your best, usually meeting your pals at some prearranged spot to start your walk on what was termed the 'monkey run'. This was a stretch of road, usually the main street, where hundreds of girls and boys would walk up and down, down and up, stopping here and there to talk to someone you knew, then if you liked each other, you would leave your respective company and go off together. If you were absent from the 'monkey run' the following Sunday, the others guessed you were going steady and your Sundays would be spent with your girl, maybe in the park or a ramble in the hills.

I entered the world in this environment, in one such cottage on the wrong side of the track, opposite the noisy and smelly gasworks giving off its fumes of gas and oxide, with the noise of its pumping machine going by day and by night. You entered the cottage through a latched door, the latch hurting your thumb as you pressed it down, being careful not to put your foot on the 'dolly-stoned' step that Mam always seemed to have just done together with the window sill. You were then in the living-room, its uneven flagged floor sparsely covered with oil-cloth. An old and heavy dresser leaned at an angle near the wall, causing any ornament on there to slide to the back when any heavy horse and cart passed by. An equally heavy carved-leg table with castors, its top highly scrubbed, stood in the centre of the room, together with four wooden chairs. On either side of the room were two not very good easy chairs, facing the blackleaded fireplace. It shone so much, you could see your face in it. A coal fire, backed up with coke was its only heating. On the hob stood a big, black, sooty kettle, that seemed forever boiling, beneath a high mantelpiece fringed with a piece of velvet with tassels. This held the family's portraits of Mam and Dad, brothers and sisters. Dad in uniform and surrounded by the flags of allied nations was prominent in the centre—quite handsome. Mam was lovely too. I would gaze at her and wish I could have known her then. Dad's clay pipes and thick twist tobacco were next to the photographs, also Mam's little tin where she saved her pennies.

The kitchen was a free-for-all affair, a cookhouse, wash-house and bathroom, all in one. In a hole under the stairs we kept the coal. A very large wooden-roller mangle with its dolly tub and dolly stood next to the cooker. It was a big iron monstrosity that I never seemed able to reach. It stood next to the cooker so that Mam could keep her eyes on whatever she was cooking while she washed. Close by was the 'slop stone', about three inches deep, where everyone in the house had to wash and where all the kids were bathed.

A big brass tap attached to a very loose lead pipe served it with its cold water supply, so often dreaded by us as children when Mam gave us a bath—or should I say wash down? The cold flannel held under the tap touched our bodies and took our breath away and left our teeth chattering, always a frightening ordeal. The draught from the back door didn't help us either.

'Don't be daft,' Mam would say if we started to cry, 'it'll harden you.'

Such was the relief when at last, the towel was wrapped round you and you ran into the front where the fire was, to stand on the rug and let the warm creep back into our small bodies.

The back door, that lifted up as you opened it, led into a large communal back yard used by a dozen or more families and their pets, dogs, cats and hens, that helped to make it dirtier than it was. Clothes lines criss-crossed the yard from all angles, held up in the middle by large props. When people's washing was hung out, it was very hard to find your way to the lavatory. It usually caused a row with someone if you as much as touched the washing.

'Watch the bloody washin', will you?' someone would shout out. 'Do yer think I've nowt else to do but wash bloody clothes for yer to dirty?'

Not knowing where the shouting was coming from or who it was shouting, you would keep hidden amongst the washing and shout back,

'Shut up, yer old bat. I'm not touchin' yer old washin'—if yer can call it that.' Then you'd make a dash for the lavatory without being seen, and once there, you could still hear the voice of some angry woman shouting,

'I know it's you, you cheeky little sod. You'll get the back of my hand if I come out there.'

The trouble was, when I'd finished, I had to shout to Mam for some paper and the woman would know who it was then.

15

Back in the house, there were thirteen steep, wooden, creaky stairs that led to the bedrooms. The back one was for Mam and Dad and the front one was our's (my brothers and sisters and me). We managed somehow through different stages of growing up. A very large iron bed with brass knobs dominated the room and was used by the lads. A three-quarter size bed in the far corner was for the two young girls. The eldest girl, the oldest child in the family lived with her aunties who were quite well off. To me she was very lovely and I looked up to her with pride and admiration as I grew up. She was quite some woman by the time I was eleven years old.

Under the iron bed with its brass knobs was kept a bucket that we used as a 'piss pot', sometimes used until it over-flowed, then God help the one who was to blame for it if Dad found out. With Mam, we'd get a good shouting at, but with Dad, anything could happen and usually did—a good thrashing. 'Leave him alone, Jack,' Mam would say, trying to shield you, 'he's only a child.' That didn't stop Dad. You would get the good hiding that wasn't forgotten in a hurry, then to top it all, you would be made to clean the mess up.

The walls of the room were whitewashed, year in and year out, layer upon layer that caused the plaster to bulge and crack under the weight. This made an ideal place for the bugs to breed. As a child, I would watch them dart across the wall, when I lay in bed at night, from the light into the shadow, caused by the flickering candle that stood in a saucer. They seemed to be waiting for the candle to go out, then in complete darkness, they would attack the sleeping children for their food, blood; then before dawn, they would scurry back to the crack in the wall. We as children had to live with this as part of our life, and accepted the bugs as if they had a right to be there. We knew no better. How did a child think? It is only when you grow up to be a man that you realize the unfairness of life; not through the fault of your parents, not in my case anyway. My Dad worked hard and my mother was good. She was clean and scrubbed and scrubbed until her hands were raw.

Yes, I and my kind lived and struggled through the environment not knowing how the other half lived. This was how it was and this was how it would be. To be poor and humble was to be blessed; at least, this is what we were taught at school and in church. But I saw how the priest would bow and shake hands with the well-off at church as they left after a service, while we passed by, unnoticed.

It was the same at school. It was the better-off children who sat for their 'county-scholarship', not me and my kind. We didn't have to be educated, but they did. Yet even in those times, someone was trying to help the poor. I found this at school when I got a small sandwich of brown bread and a small bottle of milk. Our names were called out for this privilege of getting the sandwiches and milk, and I felt the eyes of others on me as I went from my class, feeling very embarrassed. I felt alone, although other children's names were called out.

All this was endured; yet, through the eyes of a child, there was happiness, happiness so complete, I never thought about my being poor, or that my pals were poor too.

I loved the fairs that visited the town twice a year, the bonfire nights with roasted potatoes and treacle toffee, the fireworks that someone would have, even if I didn't. Then there were the carnivals—what a day for the young and old alike, when the sun shone brightly and the jazz bands, the costumes, the floats and horses in all their finery in a never-ending procession through the main streets to the park where the prizes would be awarded. Afterwards, it was the judging of the best decorated street, one competing against the other, where the people had worked so hard for a couple of days to have them ready. Every home did their own, but joined up to put up the streamers and banners. The day wouldn't have been complete without a street tea-party.

I also loved to play whip the top. Crack went the whip and the top spun. I'd have a good game of marbles, sometimes losing the lot to my opponent. When this happened, out I would go with my stick and hoop, up this street and up that street until I could run no further. All this amounted to my happiness.

Sadness came in small ways, as a good hiding and being sent to bed without your tea—that was my sadness. Worse still was the ordeal that often happened at school. Being pulled from my desk, the teacher grabbing hold of my ear or hair and taking me to the blackboard.

'You weren't paying attention, were you?' she would bark. 'Then do the sum on the board.'

I stared at my teacher, holding my ear that she had squeezed so hard. She handed me the chalk that I took in a trembling hand, and with my other hand I was trying to hide the tear in my trousers, held together with a safety pin. When I stretched up to the blackboard, the tear would open and expose my bare bottom, for underpants I didn't have. When the girls in the class saw this, they would snigger, making me more frustrated, and then I wouldn't be able to do the sum. That was a child's sadness. It was my sadness.

One way or another life went on through my childhood, through the years of the depression, seeing my brothers being humiliated by the 'means test', my leaving school a bit of a dunce, not knowing arithmetic or English as it should be spoken. I could never get the right job because of this. Yet, was I a dunce when I knew the catechism at church off by heart and from cover to cover. I could say mass in Latin as good as any learned priest. No, I wasn't a dunce in that, but in what really mattered in real life, education that I was deprived of. There would, it seemed be only manual work for such as me and other lads like me. I never dreamt at the time that I would have to fight in a world war—just like my dad. The year 1919 when I was born meant nothing to me. But I do recollect incidents when I was eight years old in 1927. It is here sometime in that year that I start my story.

Chapter Two

SCARLET FEVER

I was playing in the back yard with my pal Bernard, engrossed in a game of marbles, when my Mam called out 'Joe' in a high-pitched voice.

'Your mam's calling thee Joe,' Bernard said.

'I know she is,' I replied. 'Let's finish the game first', flicking a marble into the hole near the wall.

'I won't call you again, you little devil,' Mam shouted. 'Come here when I call you.'

I flicked another marble into the hole.

'I've beat thee,' I said as I grabbed all the marbles and stuffed them in my pocket until it bulged. Then I ran towards the back door where Mam was standing. I stood well back as if I was expecting Mam to take a swing at me, my knee-length stockings hanging around my ankles, with two big holes showing in the heels.

I wiped my running nose on the sleeve of my jersey, at the same time sniffing hard.

'What do you want, Mam?' I asked.

'Just look at the state of you,' Mam said. 'You're a dirty little devil. You can't keep clean for five minutes.'

'I've been playing marbles, Mam,' I said, taking another wipe at my nose.

'I'll play marbles if I get hold of thee,' Mam said, coming forward as if to smack me. The sixpence fell out of her hand.

'Now if that's lost, you'll get a good hiding. Find it,' Mam said. 'Then go to butcher's and get a sheep's head for your dad's dinner, and tell him to split it, and some pot herbs from Mr. Lister's.'

'Go inside first, then I'll go,' I said.

'You'd better,' Mam replied, as she went in muttering.

'Can't see it, Bernard,' I said.

'See what?' he asked.

'That bloomin' tanner. Here it is, I've found it,' I said as I ran off with arms outstretched pretending to be an aeroplane. Bernard did the same and followed me, zigzagging down the road, then we took a swing round a lamp post, climbed the high wall running round the gasworks and walked along its whole length, jumping off at the end.

'Come on,' I said to Bernard, 'I'll race thee to butcher's.' I set off unfairly with Bernard close behind.

Quite a few people were being served as I pushed my way in between them to the front, until my face was level with the highly scrubbed counter, my grubby hands resting on it. I gazed in wonder at the whole cows that hung from a rail on big hooks. My eyes wandered round at all the meat displayed as I shuffled my feet in the sawdust that covered the floor. There, besides the whole cows were sheep and pigs, all waiting to be carved up by the butcher's knife. Pigs' heads with an orange in their mouth seemed to be staring at me, as if they would come alive at any minute. A man, in a crisp white apron and straw hat was busy hanging up chickens with their heads and feathers on.

I was brought back to earth by the butcher with a large knife in his hand. He looked so big and menacing like that as I gazed up at him.

'Take those dirty hands off my counter, young fellow m'lad,' he said, pointing at me with the knife.

I quickly pulled them away.

'Excuse me, madam,' the butcher said to the woman he had just been serving. 'I'll just get rid of these little fellows.'

'Yes, you had better,' she said, giving me a look over glasses.

'What do you want, lad?' the butcher said.

'A sheep's head please, sir,' I said nervously.

'A sheep's head, ay,' he repeated, and I nodded.

'Right, just stand back there while I get it for you,' he said as he went into the back of the shop. He was back in a few seconds with the sheep's head wrapped up.

'Will you split it for me, please?'

'What?'

'Will you split it so me mam can put it in pan?'

The butcher muttered something and went back to put the cleaver through the head. The other customers laughed. The butcher returned quickly.

'Here,' he said, handing me the bundle, 'threepence.' I gave him the sixpence and when I got my change, I just ran. Bernard was outside and ran with me, down the main street and into the greengrocer's. Both of us were out of breath.

'Steady on you two before you do some damage. What do you want?'

'Some pot herbs, Mr. Lister, please,' I asked breathlessly, 'for me mam.'

'Keep you hands in your pockets, then, while I see what I've got,' Mr. Lister remarked.

Bernard and I did as we were told as Mr. Lister went round collecting celery tips, bits of carrots and the like. I still held the sheep's head firmly under my arm. Bernard and I watched Mr. Lister. He never took his eyes off us. But we just gazed at the abundance of fruit, smelling its aroma. As Mr. Lister handed the bag to me and said, 'There you are young Joe, that'll be threepence,' I said, 'Have you any rotten apples please?' Mr. Lister shook his head and smiled. 'I don't have rotten apples in this shop, but here you are,' and he handed me and Bernard an apple each.

'Ta, Mr. Lister,' we both said as we grasped the apples. We looked at each other and said 'Cheerio' to Mr. Lister. Then we walked out of the shop, taking a big bite out of the juicy apples.

'Last one home's a cissy,' Bernard shouted and set off running up our street.

'I'd have beat thee only for carrying this lot,' I shouted at Bernard as we reached our door. 'Wait there till I take these into me mam. Here you are, Mam,' I shouted into the kitchen, as I put the stuff on the table. 'I'm going out to play now.'

'Be in for yer tea,' Mam called out, 'and keep away from ten-foot lodge and that dirty tip. Do you hear now?'

'Yes, Mam,' I shouted back as I went off to play.

It was about six o'clock that evening. Mam was busy getting the tea ready. Dad was sitting in his armchair reading his paper, his sixpenny Woolworth glasses perched on his nose. As the older lads came in from work, they were laughing and pushing each other as they went into the kitchen to wash their hands.

'Hello, Mam; hello, Dad,' they said as they went through. They were still having fun and a bit of horseplay as they each tried to be first to wash their hands.

'Can't you be quiet in there, you lads?' Mam called out. 'Yer dad's trying to read his paper.'

Mam said this, knowing that it would save trouble. Dad soon got annoyed if there was any shouting when he was reading his newspaper.

'That smells good, Mam,' the lads chorused as they came out of the kitchen, wiping their hands on one towel that had seen better days.

'Why didn't you leave that in the kitchen?' Mam said, as Tom threw the towel on the back of a chair. 'Sit yourselves down and have this while it's hot,' she said as she placed a bowl of broth in front of each of them. 'Eat some bread with it,' she said as they began to tuck in.

'Is there any marg, Mam?' one of them asked.

'No there isn't,' Mam replied, 'you don't need it with broth now, do you?'

'I don't know. Some people get butter on their bread, ne'er mind marg,' he said.

Dad looked up again, glaring over his glasses.

22

'Get your tea and shut up or you'll get bugger all.'

Silence fell over them as they got on with their tea. Mam was the peacemaker when she said to Dad,

'Do you want some broth now, Jack?'

'Aye,' he replied, 'Leave some to cool for me.'

Jim who was thirteen years old, came in for his tea.

'I'm hungry, Mam,' he said, 'What is it?' as he looked over John's shoulder into his basin.

'It's broth,' Mam replied. 'Now go and wash your hands before you come to table. Come on you two,' Mam said to my two young sisters who were playing on the rug. 'I'll get you up the dancers. Say goodnight and God bless.'

When Mam came downstairs after putting them to bed, she said, 'It's time our Joe was in, it's gone half past six.'

'He'll be in when he's hungry,' Frank said.

'He'd better be,' Mam answered.

After tea was finished, Frank and John went out. Dad had gone to the pub and Tom was sitting on the floor, a shoe last between his legs, trying to mend his shoes. Mam was busy tidying up.

'Will you be long at that, Tom?' Mam said, pausing in her work.

'No, I've nearly finished,' Tom replied, 'Why?'

'Would you mind just having a look for our Joe? It's gone eight o'clock. You don't know what devilment he's up to.'

'I'll go now,' Tom said, pulling his shoe off the last and looking at it with admiration. 'That's a good job, although I say it myself. Very good,' he said again, putting the shoe on his foot. Tom got his jacket that was hanging up behind the front door. Putting it on, he said, 'I'm going now, Mam. I'll have a look round ten-foot fields. He usually plays there.' With that, he set off up the street.

'Have you seen our Joe?' Tom said to a lad as he was passing the log yard.

'Yes, mister,' the boy replied. 'He's on tip with Bernard

Moran and some other lads. We've been lookin' for coins.'

'Thanks,' Tom replied as he quickened his pace.

Mam was blackleading the fireplace on her knees when Tom walked in carrying me on his shoulders. Getting up off her knees, the brush still in her hand and a black smudge on her nose, she came over to where we were.

'Where have you been till now, you little devil?' Mam shouted at me, pulling me off Tom's shoulders and pushing me over to the fireplace. 'Get undressed right now, you don't deserve any tea. I've a good mind to put you up those dancers without any.' Mam barked at me and smacked my bottom.

'Don't hit him, Mam, he doesn't seem well.'

'I'll well him,' Mam replied, as she pulled off my jersey.

'I feel sick, Mam,' I said.

'So you should,' Mam shouted, 'staying out till this time. Yer dad would kill yer if he knew. Just look at the state of you.' She pulled off my shoes. 'You're all wet. You've been in t' ten-foot lodge again, after me tellin' you not to . . .'

I stood there with bowed head looking so sorrowful, my trousers, held up with braces, hanging below my knees, tears leaving a streak on my cheeks as they rolled freely down my face.

'Come on now, old lad,' Tom said, coming over to me, putting his arms round me and kneeling on one knee. 'What's wrong with yer?'

I leaned my head on Tom's shoulder.

'I feel sick,' I said and sobbed bitterly. Tom held me close.

Mam came in from the kitchen carrying a bowl of warm water and a towel, which she placed on the rug.

'Bring me a flannel, will you, Tom? And that piece of carbolic soap, it's on the slop stone,' Mam said. 'I'd forget me head if it was loose, I've so much to think about with all of ye. Thanks,' Mam said to Tom as he handed her the soap and flannel. 'You are hot and feverish, love,' Mam said as she

24

touched my little body and began to wash my face.

I cried more and said, 'I feel sick, Mam.'

'I'll soon have you better. When I've bathed you, I'll get you a powder and put you up to bed. Tom, you'd better get me a Fennings fever cure from bottom shop, you'll get a penny in my purse on dresser.'

'I'll get it, Mam,' Tom said as he went out.

Then as Mam rubbed me down with the towel, she noticed red patches mostly on my bottom.

'You are sick, love, aren't yer? God love you,' Mam said.

'Here you are, Mam,' Tom said, as he handed Mam the powder. Mam took it and poured it on to a spoon with a touch of cold tea.

'Open yer mouth, love,' she said as she held my nose between her fingers. 'Open wide.' Mam put the powder in. 'Close your mouth and swallow and drink this,' she said, holding a cup to my lips. I pulled a funny face as I swallowed the powder. It tasted awful. Mam got a clean but worn shirt from the fire-guard where it has been airing. I wasn't lucky enough to have pyjamas. In fact, the shirt must have been my brother Jim's as it reached my knees and the sleeves hung below my hands.

Mam picked me up and carried me upstairs and put me in the brass-knobbed bed. Covering me up, she lit the candle in the saucer.

'I'll bring you up an overcoat to put over you too,' she said. 'You must keep warm. That powder will sweat you, and don't forget, if you are sick, use the bucket.' She pulled the bucket from under the bed.

'Can you leave the candle lit? Just for a little while?' I asked Mam.

'Alright, just for a little while. Now say your prayers and ask God to make you better,' Mam said.

'Only God can make you better,' I said.

'That's right love, only God,' Mam replied. 'Now make the sign of the cross with me. In the name of the Father and of the

Son and of the Holy Ghost, Amen.'

I repeated it after Mam, then quite suddenly I said,

'There are no real ghosts, are there Mam? Only the Holy Ghost.'

'That's right love, just the Holy Ghost. Now say your prayers and ask God to make you well,' Mam said.

When I finished Mam said,

'That's a good boy, love. Now try and go to sleep.' She gave me a kiss and said, 'Goodnight and God bless.'

'Goodnight and God bless, Mam,' I said, putting my arms round her neck and giving her a hug.

The flame of the candle flickered as I lay there with the clothing pulled up to my nose and I watched the shadows dancing on the wall. Just the noise of the pumping machine at the gasworks and the faint sound of voices from someone downstairs, told me I wasn't alone. How long I was awake, I don't know, but sleep overtook me.

I heard Mam calling the lads for work the next morning.

'Try not to waken Joe when you get out,' she said. She placed her hand on my forehead.

'I'll have to get the doctor to him. He's burning up. I'll see to you, love, when I get the lads their breakfast and see them off to work.'

'Can I have a drink, Mam?' I asked.

'Yes, I'll bring you one up as soon as I can,' Mam said as she went downstairs. It seemed so long before she came up with a mug of milk.

'Get up, Jim,' Mam called as she came into the room with the mug in one hand and shaking Jim with the other.

'Do you hear me, lad?' Mam repeated.

'Yea, yea, I hear yer,' Jim replied, very sleepily.

'Then get up now. You'll have to call at doctor's on yer way to school.'

Jim got up, pulled his trousers on and went downstairs.

'Here, love,' Mam said, 'sit up and take this,' offering me the mug of milk. I tried to sit up but I felt so weak, I couldn't. Mam put her hand round me and raised me up, putting the mug to my lips. I took a few small sips through cracked, dry lips.

'I don't want any more, Mam,' I said.

She seemed worried. 'Right love,' she said as she lay me down again and pulled the clothes round my shoulders. Poor Mam, she was crying.

'What are yer crying for, Mam?' I said, looking up at her.

'Me? I'm not crying, you silly,' she replied and she wiped her eyes with the back of her hand. 'I'll go and see our Jim off to school,' she said and went out of the room and downstairs.

'Aren't yer washed yet?' Mam said to Jim, who was still standing on the rug in front of the fire, scratching himself.

'I can't find me stockings,' Jim replied.

'Yer old enough to find 'em. I can't keep running after yer all,' Mam said. 'Don't yer think I've enough to do looking after yer all and your brother poorly too? Now just get a move on before yer dad comes in. He'll be across from work soon for his cup of tea.'

It didn't take Jim long to find his socks and get ready. He was at the table having his breakfast when Dad walked in, a large lump of coal tucked in his jacket. He walked right through and put the coal under the stairs.

'How's young Joe, Lizzie?' Dad asked as he walked back into the house.

'He's not well at all,' Mam replied handing Dad a cup of tea, some of which he poured into his saucer, blew on it, then gulped it down.

'Are you getting doctor to him?' Dad asked, finishing his tea and putting the cup and saucer on the table.

'Yes, Jim's calling on his way to school,' Mam replied.

'He'll be alreet, you'll see, Lizzie,' Dad said. 'I'll have to

27

get back to work now.' Dad walked to the door, peering up and down the street to see if any boss was about.

'All clear,' he shouted, 'I'll see yer,' and he darted across the road and into the works gates.

'I'm off now, Mam,' Jim shouted, putting on his cap.

'Right,' replied Mam. 'Don't forget to ask doctor to call. Tell him it's yer brother Joe, he's feverish.'

'Right-oh, Mam,' Jim shouted, and he ran off.

I must have fallen asleep for I didn't hear Mam getting my young sisters up out of bed.

It was around eleven o'clock when the doctor came.

'Which one is it, Mrs. Murphy?'

'It's Joe, doctor, he's upstairs,' Mam said, wiping her hands on her apron. 'He's not well at all.'

The doctor followed Mam upstairs.

'The doctor's here to see you, love,' Mam said, as she wakened me.

I looked up with sleepy eyes. The doctor looked like a giant standing there, but I was too sick to be frightened.

'Open your mouth,' the doctor said, as he stood shaking a thermometer, looked at it and placed it in my mouth. Then he lifted my arm and took my pulse. I held the glass tube between tight lips and stared at the doctor. There was silence as he gazed at his pocket watch.

'That's a good lad,' he said, taking the instrument from my mouth and looking at it.

'Hmmmm, yes,' he remarked putting the thermometer away. He pulled the bedclothes down and lifted my shirt, pressing his fingers on my tummy.

'You are Joe, are you?' the doctor asked as he covered me up again. I nodded my head. Then turning to Mam, who was standing at the foot of the bed, looked worried and said to her,

'I'm afraid Joe is quite ill. It's scarlet fever. I will arrange for him to go to hospital. In the meantime, keep your other

28

children away from him and keep him warm.'

'Right, doctor,' Mam said as they went downstairs. Their voices grew fainter.

It was about two o'clock. Dad was home from work and was sitting reading the racing paper. Mam had taken my young sisters to Mrs. O'Brien's to mind for her when Uncle Bill called (he was a runner for a betting shop).

"Ast owt today, Jack?' Uncle Bill asked as he rushed in.

'Give me bloody time, will tha?' Dad said as he began to write out his slip (a sixpenny each way double). 'Here, take that, Bill.'

Uncle Bill took the slip and put it in his pocket. He said, 'I believe young Joe isn't well, Jack?'

'No, he isn't,' Dad replied. 'He's going into hospital today. Doctor's bin, he thinks it's scarlet fever.'

'What!' Uncle Bill said with surprise. 'That's bloody catching, i'nt it?'

'I think so,' Dad replied, 'but only if——'; but before Dad completed what he was saying, Uncle Bill had gone. Dad had to laugh as he got up and went to the door.

'He went quick,' Dad said to himself and he saw Uncle Bill at the top of the street. Mam was coming down the street as Dad stood at the door. When she got near, she said,

'Th'ambulance should be here soon, Jack. I do wish they'd hurry up. It's worrying, all this waiting, and lad so sick upstairs. They'll look after him, won't they, Jack?'

'Course they'll bloody look after him, it's a hospital i'nt it?'

'I know, but I'll miss him,' Mam said as she went indoors. She was going upstairs when Dad shouted,

'It's here, Lizzie.'

'Send them up when they come in,' Mam said.

The ambulance stopped at the door and two men in uniform got out. One of them had a red blanket over one arm.

29

'Are we at the right address?' one of them said to Dad as they came to the door.

'Are yer from fever hospital?' Dad asked.

'We are.'

'Then it's right place. He's upstairs.' Dad went on, 'You can go up.'

'You'll look after him?' Mam said to the men as they wrapped me in a blanket.

'We will, missus, don't you worry. He'll be alreet, won't you, lad?' The man picked me up and carried me to the ambulance. I felt too weak and ill to worry where I was going to. Just my eyes showed in the red bundle, but I saw Mam crying bitterly. (How many times had Mam cried in her life, for her children, I wonder.)

As I was carried out of the house to the ambulance, I could see groups of people standing around holding their children by the hand. They stood well back as if they were afraid I could realize what they would be saying—'It's Joe Murphy, he's got scarlet fever, its contagious, we'd better not get too near.'

The ambulance door opened and as I was carried in, to be laid on a bed of some sort, the man carrying me sat by its side, saying, 'You'll be alright son, you'll be alright.'

I felt so alone. Before the doors closed, I strained my head to see my mam. She stood there, her handkerchief up to her eyes. Dad was by her side with no visible signs of emotion, but dads don't cry, I thought. The doors closed and the ambulance began to move off. The windows were dark, I couldn't see anything then, but I looked back with tears.

'Well that's that,' Mam said to Dad as they went indoors.

'I wonder what the lads will say when they come home from work?'

'What the hell can they say?' Dad asked. 'Just get on with yer work. The lad's gone, hasn't he? You've got the others to

30

think about now.' Mam just looked at Dad but didn't reply. She understood him and I'm sure this was his way of showing how he felt. He never showed any emotion, but who could tell how he felt inside?

'I'll go for the girls,' Mam said, putting on her coat. Dad remained silent, just looking at the paper and probably wishing the pub was open.

'Are yer there, Nellie?' Mam called as she stood at Mrs. O'Brien's door.

'Come in, Lizzie,' was the reply.

As Mam walked in, Mrs. O'Brien was standing in the kitchen doorway, a big woman, compared to Mam. She stood there with her arms folded across her very large bosom; her apron, tied at the waist, was so long that you could just see her highly polished brass-tipped clogs.

'Sit yerself down, lass, I'll get yer a cup of tea.'

This sympathy shown to Mam was enough to start her crying, as she sat there, looking at her two little girls playing on the rug.

'Now then, Lizzie,' Mrs. O'Brien said, as she walked in with two cups of tea, 'stop that crying. Your lad'll be alreet now he's in th'ospital.' Mam sipped her tea.

'Have they been good, Nellie?' she asked.

'Good did you say? I wish I'd had a dozen like 'em. I'll say this, Lizzie, you may shed some tears for them, but by God, it's worth a few tears to have a family like yours. You bring 'em up good, every single one of 'em. You know, we've never been blessed with children, Tom and me, but if we had, we'd have asked for nothing more than for 'em to be like yours. I love every one of 'em.'

'I know yer do, Nellie,' Mam said. 'Yer a good woman. Come on, you two, let's get some tea ready. Is that right time, Nellie?' Mam said, looking at the big grandfather clock.

'It's bin right time for past forty years, to my knowledge,' Mrs. O'Brien replied with a laugh.

'Right, I'll see you then,' Mam said as she took the girls by the hand and went home.

'See you Lizzie,' called Mrs. O'Brien, going to the door.

'I'll see to tea in a minute Jack,' Mam said as she walked in, but Dad never heard her—he was fast asleep in the chair.

'Now be good little girls. Don't make a noise and waken yer Daddy while I get tea ready.'

Mam got the table set, got the girls their tea, and was waiting for Jim to come home from school to go to the chip shop. The mill buzzer sounded as Mam went to the door to see if she could see our Jim.

'There he is, the little monkey,' said Mam to herself. 'Just watch him strolling up as if he had all night. Jim,' she shouted as only Mam could shout. She could be heard a mile away. Well, Jim heard all right; he started to run home.

'Where have you been till now? School's been over ages ago. I've a good mind to clout you one.'

'I've only been playing with lads,' Jim replied as he dashed past Mam.

'Get your hands washed and go to chip shop for lads' tea. Hurry yerself up,' Mam shouted, 'they'll be in any minute. The basin and money's on t' table.'

Jim washed his hands in quick time, grabbed the money and basin, and was nearly out the door when Mam called him back.

'I haven't told you what I want yet.'

'I forgot, Mam,' Jim said.

'Get two bean mixtures, one pea mixture and threepence worth of chips. Oh, and get a fish for yer dad. Have you got that?' Jim repeated the order to Mam and then went, Mam shouting to him to be careful with the food.

'There's a mug of tea, Jack,' Mam said as she woke Dad. Dad mumbled as he woke. 'There's your paper and I've got yer a fish for yer tea when Jim comes back. He shouldn't be long now.'

32

'What time is it?' Dad asked.

'Quarter to six. They're coming out of mill. I'll stand at door and see if I can see lads coming.'

Dad didn't mind what she did, he was busy looking at the paper to see if he had won on the horses. Mam was kept busy saying 'Hello' to everyone that passed coming from work. I think she knew everybody and everybody knew Mam. This is what it was like in those days; in your town, everyone seemed to know each other and they had a great community spirit.

'They're comin' now,' Mam said. They always walked home together after their hard day's work in the spinning room, their cloth caps at a jaunty angle and carrying their dinner basins wrapped in red-and-white dotted handkerchiefs. They saw Mam standing at the door and waved to her.

'How's our Joe?' was the first thing they asked as they came to the door.

Mam said, 'He's in th'ospital.'

'What?' they chorused.

'He went about three o'clock to isolation hospital. He's got scarlet fever, doctor said.'

'Where the hell's he picked that up?' Tom asked.

'Look,' Mam said, 'go on in and get washed. Yer tea'll be here in a few minutes. Go on,' Mam repeated, giving one of them a push.

'Hello, Dad,' each one said as they went through to the kitchen.

'Hello,' Dad replied, 'You heard about Joe, then?'

'Yes, Dad; Mam just towd us.'

'It's a rum do,' Dad said, then started to read his paper. The lads got washed and were just sitting down when Jim came in with their tea.

'Good,' Mam said, 'just in time.'

There wasn't much said at the tea-table that night. Jim ate his tea quickly and went out. Frank got ready and went to the billiard hall. Tom went to see his girlfriend, Nellie. John knew what he was doing, he was going to play some records for Mam and Dad.

'Aren't yer going out tonight, John?' Mam asked him as he sat reading.

'No, not tonight, Mam. I was hoping you and Dad might like to listen to some records. It would take yer mind off things, that's unless Dad's going out to pub for a drink.'

'No,' said Dad. 'Mam can get me a drink in jug from Off Licence.'

'Good,' said John. 'I've got a new record of John McCormack you might like to hear.'

'When do you and Frank go to night school?'

'Not till tomorrow night, Mam,' replied John.

'I'll just slip up and tell Mrs. Bennett about Joe. She'll wonder where he is when he doesn't call to see her.'

'Don't be long, Mam, will yer, then we can get started.'

'I'll only be a few minutes,' Mam replied.

I was about six weeks in the fever hospital. During that time, Mam and Dad visited me twice but I could only see them through the window as visitors were not allowed in. This was usually a crying session when it was time to go. Then Mrs. Bennett came one day and brought me sweets and cakes which were divided amongst the other children. Mrs. Bennett wasn't a relation, but my fairy godmother; that is what I called her, as she was so good to me. As a baby, when I had started to walk, and although she lived about six houses away, it was her house I first went to. From the very first day I toddled in, I became attached to her and her husband, or should I say they became attached to me. Why I never knew, for they never had any children of their own.

It was often said in conversation over the years that I was attracted to the parrot that they kept; this could very well have been, but all the same, no matter what took me in as a child, I came to love them as I grew up and they loved me. The attachment grew stronger with Mrs. Bennett after her husband died.

I would be about seven years old when it happened. I had just visited him, one lunchtime. Mrs. Bennett was at the mill and Mr. Bennett had retired. He was sitting in his rocking chair and I was talking to him when he fell over and on to the floor. I was frightened when he wouldn't speak to me.

'Mr. Bennett,' I called, 'speak to me Mr. Bennett.'

I started to cry and ran out and down to my house.

'Mam, Mam,' I shouted excitedly, 'Mr. Bennett's sick. He's fallen on the floor near the fire. He wouldn't speak to me.' Mam just said, 'Good God,' and hurried out with me running past her.

'Hurry Mam, hurry,' I said.

'Tell Mrs. O'Brien to come quick,' Mam replied.

'Mrs. O'Brien,' I called out, from her doorstep, 'Mam wants you. Mr. Bennett is sick.'

Mam and Mrs. O'Brien did what they could for Mr. Bennett but he died; he had had a stroke.

This was how the attachment between Mrs. Bennett and myself grew, and why she was now visiting me at the hospital. She also brought me a pair of trousers and a jersey, my coming home outfit.

The big day arrived at last—I was going home. There I was at the annexe window, dressed up in my new trousers and jersey waiting and watching for my mam and dad. I had been standing at the window from nine o'clock and it was now quarter past eleven. I wondered where they were; it seemed like an eternity as I watched the taxis come and go.

'Aren't your mam and dad here yet, Joe?' a nurse asked as she passed. I turned from the window and shook my head; my bottom lip started to quiver which the nurse noticed.

'They'll not be long now,' she said. 'You're not going to cry, are you?' I again shook my head.

'You don't want your parents to see you crying now, do you?'

'No,' I said, shaking my head again.

'That's a good boy, Joe. Now, I'll bring you a nice drink and a biscuit. I'm sure you're hungry, aren't you?' the nurse asked.

'Yes, I am,' I said with downcast eyes.

The nurse hadn't gone long before I heard her shout, 'Joe, Joe.' I ran to the door leading into the corridor and opened it. The nurse was coming towards me saying,

'You'll have to miss that drink I promised you, Joe. Run along, your Mam's waiting for you,' giving me a playful smack on my bottom.

As I ran down the corridor, I saw my mam with her arms outstretched. I ran right into them and hugged her.

'Hello, love,' Mam said, giving me a kiss and holding me tightly.

'Goodbye, Joe,' the nurse said as she put her hand on my head.

'Goodbye, nurse,' I replied with a big smile.

'Don't forget to wave to your friends as you go. There they are,' the nurse said, pointing to a window.

I saw them, standing there in their hospital dressing gowns. They were waving, most of them with sorrowful faces. I must confess, at my age of eight years, I was happy. I didn't realize what their feelings were as I smiled and waved back. I was going home, at last.

Chapter Three

THE MILLS CLOSE

My life from then on was reasonably happy. Jim had left school and was working in a cotton mill; a very hot, sultry weaving shed, carrying bobbins. A hard job for a mere boy of fourteen years, a boy clever enough to be going to grammar school, to be properly educated and to be given that chance in life he deserved.

Like me and my brothers, Jim would be a pawn in life's game of chess to be moved and taken by the men in charge of this human game.

John and Frank were working full time, but they had the sense to try to educate themselves, by religiously going to night school. They didn't intend to work in a spinning room in the cotton mill for the rest of their lives. They intended to make the grade and move up in life, do something themselves that was denied them by others.

John himself was a very good cricketer, as good as, if not better than anyone in the town. But he could never get the chance to play for the Town Team. He was from the wrong side of the track.

Tom was more on the carefree side. He was different, I think; a little more like Dad in his temperament, liked to gamble, win or lose, but he was generous and a good brother and also worked hard.

My sister Marion was the eldest. A lovely girl, also working in the mill, she loved life and loved dancing. Many's the competition she entered and won; and, as I remember, she had many admirers and she was runner-up in a National Beauty Contest.

My young sisters had started school. I usually got the job of taking these two, Hilda and Kathleen, out for a walk, a task I didn't like as it stopped me from playing with the lads.

I remember one time when I had to take them out with me, I was annoyed, and when I got to the park, I left them to play on the wheel by themselves while I played with some lads. I was to wish I'd never done that for Hilda had fallen off the spinning wheel and hurt her mouth badly, her two front teeth getting damaged. It's no wonder I remembered this incident, I got a good hiding.

My youngest brother, and the last born, had only just arrived into this world.

As I said, life was quite enjoyable as the months and years went by.

Now I was near on twelve years of age and just around the corner was the depression, 1930.

'Hard times for you, these words were said' were to come true, not just for me and my family alone, but for thousands and thousands of people.

The prospect of the workhouse loomed near, that large cold grey building, hidden behind a high wall and trees. It preyed on the minds of a lot of people and, I'm sorry to say, many a poor soul finished up there. The first indication I got of these hard times was when my brother came home from work one day. Mam was at the door looking out for them coming up the street. She noticed some very glum faces as the workers passed.

'Hello, Mary,' Mam called out to someone she knew.

'Hello, Lizzie,' came the reply, 'bad news tonight.'

'What's that?' Mam said.

'They've only put mill on three days,' Mary replied, 'things are getting bad.'

Mam went inside to see to the tea. Dad was working until ten o'clock.

'Hello, Mam,' they said as they walked in the house and through to the kitchen, but Mam didn't answer; she just looked at them as if expecting them to say something about the mill. They were at the slop stone washing their hands when Mam went in.

'What's this I hear about mill?' she asked. 'Is it true you're going on three days from next week?'

'Ay, it's true, Mam,' Tom said, 'but it's only temporary so they say. Don't you go worrying, Mam, we'll manage somehow. Things look black now, but they'll pick up, you'll see.'

How wrong Tom was, for in the course of events that followed, things were to go far beyond anyone's imagination. The mills closed, first one and then another. The workers were paid up and the gates closed, never to reopen. Dejected men and women, boys and girls—what was to happen to them? The heart was being ripped out of the town. A long blast on the mill buzzer denoted its closure; it was like hearing its death knell, like the bugler blowing the Last Post. It wasn't very long before the last mill closed.

These mills, where most of the town's population worked, and which had once stood so majestically, puffing out smoke from their tall chimneys and seen as living symbols of employment, were now dead. It was sign on the 'dole' daily; the queues grew longer as other industries were affected. Each day that passed brought more bad news. Every town in the north-west and farther was now affected.

My brothers tramped here and there for work, but it was the same wherever they went—'no vacancies'—these notices were on every gate.

One day, when my brothers went to sign on, they were told on reaching the counter, 'Nothing for you'. They were dumbstruck. What would they do now? They argued in vain and were just told that instead of 'dole', it was a 'means test'; that meant that if one wage was going into the house, no matter how large the family, that was enough. Everything fell now on Dad's shoulders.

I only remembered my Dad vaguely when I was eight years

old, but now at twelve years of age, I had more sense. I can recall things that happened when I was this age far better than I could at eight years of age. I can sympathize with him now, the burden he had to carry. Eleven of a family to keep, feed and clothe on one wage. What the hell had he fought a war for? Who could blame him for taking a drink and for his bad temper? To struggle and provide for this lot was certainly a feat in itself. 'Direction of labour'—my brothers had now become the pawns. Wherever a little work had to be done, they were sent. The distance didn't matter, they still had to make their own way on foot, or if someone had an old cycle that could carry two, they were lucky.

Maybe they got a few days on the log yard or, in the winter, snow shifting. They were always thankful for that few bob to supplement Dad's wage.

I remember once, the time they were sent to plant trees somewhere on the moors. Miles away in the hills they went, in small groups, up hills and down dales, and having to set off so very early in the morning and taking only a couple of 'butties' (bread) for their lunch.

The street corner boys, as Mam called them, came into prominence. Lads and men with nothing to do, standing around all day, searching their waistcoat pockets for 'tab ends'. They seemed to get some money here and there, for the pubs were always full and blokes certainly got drunk. I think it was easier in those days as beer was stronger and you could buy three pints for one shilling.

My own life was apart from these worries as yet. My little world revolved round my pals. I only had to run indoors, grab a jam butty and go out again to play. The jam butty was always there, so why should I worry. I never noticed that Mam wasn't buying me a new pair of trousers or a pair of clogs any more, but getting them from a jumble sale instead. It was only a game to me to go and pick coal on the railway sidings. It didn't worry me to go to the butcher's for a sheep's head instead of steak, or get a ticket to go to the Christmas party for the poor; to see my poor Mam run out into the road to pick up pieces of coal that had fallen off the horse-drawn cart as it turned into the gasworks yard from the cobbled street. Mam became a master of knowing when the cart was just ready to turn, and she'd be the first out with her bucket. Sometimes it was me or Jim who had to do it with Mam standing in the doorway directing operations.

I was going to know, though, what work was like, in the form of a paper round, morning and evening. It was a long round, on the other side of the track. I delivered papers to all the big houses. I had to get up at five-thirty a.m., come summer, come winter. I was only a small lad and the paper-bag I carried was so heavy, Friday being the worst day with papers and magazines. It was so heavy that Dad made my brother Jim get up and help me before he went to do a part-time job he had got.

I was always late for school but I didn't worry when I got the cane. The few bob I earned helped my Mam. Going to school wasn't going to help me at all in the future. It was unfair to lads and girls like me. I got a lot of cane, a lot of religion but not enough help in the things that mattered to equip me for the future—education and a chance to sit my matric. Without this, I was lost and the least said about my school, the better. I looked forward and was excited when I knew that I had only a month to go before I left school, because I felt as a child that there was prejudice against my kind, just coming from working-class origin, and it was to follow me through life and prevent me from getting the work I would have liked to have done.

I left my school at long last, without ceremony.

I just wanted to get a job, any job, that would give me a wage that I could give to my Mam.

My first job I got was in a ropeworks. I got this from a customer of mine on my paper round. He owned the factory and gave me my first start. It was too far to travel, and when the chance came for another job nearer, I took it. This was on a farm about two miles from town. I had to get up at five a.m. and I never got home until around seven o'clock. I was working and the hours didn't matter; I was earning money, not much, but it helped.

A bad road accident one night nearly cost me my life. It happened one winter's night as I left the farm on my old cycle, coming down the steep unlit road. In my pocket, I carried a bottle of milk and when I came off my cycle, the bottle broke and penetrated my side. Although I was on the danger list, it was the quick attention from the ambulance men and doctor that saved my life. I never returned to work at the farm again.

My next job, after I recovered from my accident, was something that I really loved. I became a stable boy for a local firm of carriers. I had to look after six beautiful carthorses. I had to be at the stable by four-thirty a.m. It was my responsibility to feed the horses, muck them out, groom them and clean their harnesses. It was a hard job. I had to have them ready for the carters when they arrived for work. Woe betide me if they weren't ready and properly groomed; I would receive a smack round my earhole; this only happened once and I made sure it never happened again. One horse was my own personal responsibility. It was called Jimmy, a fine specimen standing sixteen hands. He was used by me as a chain-horse, that is, I had to hook it on to the shafts of the other horses to help them to pull their large loads up the very steep hills.

This, too, was a long day, and I was very tired at the end. But I knew the few bob I got helped Mam in those trying times.

I helped the coal carters to carry coal to the customers' houses and I became as expert as any man. I was only young, but I was strong and, believe me, I was just waiting my chance to get on the job of 'coal bagger' and be on man's money, as so many people were out of work.

My brothers were still searching around for jobs, and I heard some talk that they were going south, as prospects were better down there; it was a case of move or die. My brother Tom didn't want to leave. He was hoping to get a job at the gas-works. In fact, he had asked Dad to ask for him, but Dad was so proud, he wouldn't hear of it.

'No,' he said, 'I bloody won't ask for you,' when Tom mentioned it. 'Tha'll get thee own job and stand on thee own two feet', Dad said, 'I'll bow to no man.'

That statement made Tom very angry, and he vowed he would get on without anyone's help.

One day, I got my chance, through someone's misfortune. One of the carters, called 'owd Bill', a man of sixty or so, had died suddenly. This caused a vacancy, which was advertised. There must have been fifty men applying for the job, and I, a mere boy, was one of them.

'This is a man's job, lad,' I was told, 'Yer but a lad yet, and a small one at that.'

That was certainly true, I was small and young, but there was a lot at stake. I wasn't going to give up easily; my family wanted money too. The job didn't warrant an interview at the office by the directors, but by the foreman at the stables where I already worked. Outside stood a cart, loaded with coal bags, filled with coal (1 cwt). The foreman selected six men only, and he was testing them by asking each one to carry a bag of coal and tip it in the corner. Three of these men looked as if they could carry the cart as well, they were certainly big enough. They wore clogs and their trousers were held up by very broad belts. They wore thick union shirts, open at the front, showing off broad chests. Yes, they looked tough.

As each one had emptied a bag of coal, I ran forward.

'Can I have a go, Mr. B?' I said. He looked at me with surprise.

'Please, Mr. B, will you?'

'Go on, have a go and be careful.'

'I will, Mr. B, I will. Bert,' I called out to one of the carters standing in the yard. 'Put one on will you?' I said, as I put my back to the large sack on the lorry. Bert knew what I meant because he had taught me the knack of carrying sacks of coal— in fact, two at once.

Bert jumped on the lorry, and as I got my first bag in the right position, I said, 'Right'. Bert put the other bag on that, just rightly balanced, I walked to the corner and tipped them, much to the amazement of the foreman and the other men there. I know I was showing off, but it paid off. The very next morning, Mr. B said he would let the men know if they had got the job, and if looks could kill, I would have died, from the looks I got as they went away. I felt for them, of course, but it was hard times. If you didn't work you went hungry, and my family had been deprived so long.

The next morning I was told I could have the job, the wage thirty-eight shillings a week. It was hard, very hard, getting soaked to the skin, getting raw hands with the gritty, wet coal when it rained. Getting a sore back with the big lumpy coal that stuck into you and getting choked up with coal dust on the hot days. I wasn't educated, and this was my lot, just for money to help out at home.

Time went by. Eventually, Tom got a start at the gasworks. Jim, John and Frank had left home and gone south. My two young sisters would be leaving school soon and my young brother, Brian, was about nine years old. My eldest sister was married, and Dad was still working. It was easier for Mam, right enough, but she missed the lads. She went to the pictures twice a week which she liked very much, just the first house. It was only threepence to go in and things were easier now.

In the summer months, when Dad was on the early shift, he and Mam would walk up by the park and the cricket field, every night they could, then Dad would go for a pint when they returned.

I would go to the pictures or a sixpenny hop, and I also took up boxing; I only got expenses wherever I went to fight, but it was enjoyable. I also did a bit of courting, I knew plenty of girls around, but I never took anyone seriously.

In 1938, war clouds were gathering over Europe. The papers were full of stories about Hitler and the 'Nazis', but I don't think anyone took it seriously; well, I certainly didn't. Life went on as usual. Little did we know that in a few months' time, World War II would start, and once more we, the pawns in the human game, would be moved about life's chessboard. This time in a more serious game—War. But this wasn't moving just the poor, it involved everyone, rich and poor alike; that is why I didn't mind going. This war did unite us and one thing was sure, no matter what we had been through in the depression or what we had been deprived of because we were poor—even Dad who had been through the First World War and was about to see his six sons go to this one—we loved this country of ours and we intended to fight for it.

Chapter Four

THE LETTERS

The letter was on the dresser when I came in from work.

'Joe,' Mam said, 'Will you take that letter up to Dr. Hannan's when you've had your tea?'

'What letter? Who's it for?' I asked, going over to the dresser and picking it up.

'It's our Kathleen's name on it but a different address,' I said.

'It's the doctor's address and the letter must be for that young Irish girl who works for him, I'm sure. Anyhow, just go up with it and see, will you?'

'Course I will, but I need a good wash first, I'm filthy.'

'Just wash your hands first and get your tea while it's hot.'

'Yes,' I said, going into the kitchen to wash.

'I'll take it,' my sister Hilda said, as I washed my black hands under the tap.

'Ger out of it,' I shouted, flicking water at her from my fingers. 'You leave it alone.'

'I'm only codding you,' she said. 'I know you want to see what the girl's like.'

Within the hour, I was washed and tidied up and on my way to the doctor's with the letter.

'I hope it's her that comes to the door,' I thought as I pressed the doorbell and waited. The door opened.

'Can I help you?' she said with a lovely smile on her face.

'Will—er—would this be your letter?' I spluttered out. 'Is your name Kathleen?'

'It is for sure,' she answered in a soft Irish brogue. 'Why?

46

How did you get it?'

'It came to my house by mistake. You see, I've a sister called Kathleen,' I said.

'I see. Well it is very nice of you to bring it to me and I thank you,' she said as she took it from my hand, and with a smile that made my knees tremble, she began to close the door.

'Just a minute,' I said, as I put my hand on the door.

'Yes?' (She said 'yes' so beautifully.)

'Er, nothing,' I replied and I took my hand away from the door. 'It's nothing.'

'Goodnight,' she said and closed the door.

I stood absolutely stunned.

'Christ,' I said to myself, 'I've just got to date her. I've just got to. She's bloody lovely.'

With my hands in my pockets, I strolled down the street. It was a summer evening and I think everyone in the street was sitting out at their doors on little wooden buffets and chairs, enjoying the evening sun and having a chat. When I reached our door, Mam was sitting out too, talking to some of the neighbours.

'Did you give it to her?' Mam said.

'I did,' I replied, 'and I'm going to let you into a little secret, Mam.'

'A secret?' Mam said, laughing.

'Yes,' I replied, 'I'm going to marry that girl.'

You could hear Mam and the neighbours laughing a mile away.

'You can laugh as much as you like, Mam. I'm telling you, I'll marry that girl some day,' I said as I walked in the house. I don't know what made me say that to Mam, but I knew that I had fallen in love.

I was destined not to see Kathleen, or should I say not to speak to her, for quite a while, a good few months. I did see her now and then as I was passing on the coal cart. I would see her and attract her attention as I passed, by whistling or a wave, I think it embarrassed her and I don't think she knew who I was with my dirty black face. I must have frightened her.

Months went by. My brother Tom had joined the Territorial Army. John had got married, down south, and I still hadn't met Kathleen. Then the worst happened. On September 3rd, 1939, we heard the news that England was at war with Germany— World War II had started. Tom, in the Territorials, was sent to France; John had joined up; Frank and Jim followed soon after. I was given a short reprieve until February 1940.

'There's a letter for yer Joe,' Mam shouted upstairs to waken me for work.

'Right, comin',' I shouted back.

I jumped out of bed, pulled my trousers on and hurried downstairs.

'Where is it?' I said, my eyes only half open.

'It's on table in front of yer,' Mam replied, 'and get yer hands washed before yer sit down.'

'I didn't hear her, for when I picked up the letter, I saw in big black letters O.H.M.S. I opened it hurriedly.

'What is it, Joe?' Mam said, as she looked round, a long toasting fork in her hand, toasting a piece of bread.

'Go on, read it out,' she said.

My eyes scanned the letter.

'It's me calling-up papers,' I said, looking at Mam as if for help. 'Yer toast is burning, Mam. Quick,' I shouted. Smoke was pouring from what remained of the bread, which Mam quickly threw into the fire. She looked worried, and I admit I felt frightened now it had come. Talking about war was one thing, but going was another. I looked at the letter again and read it out.

'You are ordered to report for a medical at such a time on February 2nd, 1940. That's only four days, Mam'; but poor Mam didn't hear me. She was sitting in the chair crying her eyes out.

'Come on, Mam love, don't cry. Me brothers are all in th'army aren't they?'

'That's the trouble,' Mam replied, in between sobs. 'Do they have to take all me lads, do they?' I was really speechless, as I saw Mam crying like that over me.

I left her to cry as I went into the kitchen to wash and get ready for work. She was better to be left alone, she would get over it.

After I had washed and had my breakfast, Mam had got over her crying bout.

'Cheerio, Mam, see you tonight,' I said.

'Cheerio, love,' she replied.

I talked a lot at work about my medical, I even got a few tips from my customers which surprised me. At least they were concerned about me; that made me feel better.

Dad was in when I got home from work.

'Hello, Dad,' I said as I walked in. 'Did Mam tell you about me medical?'

'Ay, she did, lad, when is it?'

'Tuesday at ten-thirty a.m.,' I said.

'It's what I thowt,' Dad said, 'they'd have you next, and now it's here, we'll have to make best of it. There's a war on. Anyhow, I'm off for a drink.'

'Mam,' I said as I sat down to my tea, 'do you ever see that Irish girl from doctor's at all?'

'I saw her on Sunday running down road, going to Mass,' Mam replied.

'I would love to meet her before I go in th'army,' I said.

'That's your problem, love,' she said.

'I know that,' I replied, 'but I will meet her one day, that I do know.'

Tuesday morning arrived and I set off to my medical at Stockport full of apprehension, not knowing what to expect. I didn't have to wait long to know that I would pass A1. The place was crowded with lads around my age, going through the same routine, seeing this doctor and that doctor, like something going through a process machine.

'Any disability?'

'No, doctor.'

'Eyes all right?'

'Yes, doctor.'

'Read the notice. Move on. Next please.'

Another doctor said, 'Cough. Right. Next.'

After I had got dressed, I had to report to the man at the desk where I signed some form or other.

'You will be notified,' he said. 'Next.'

Before I knew it, I was on my way back home, wondering what it was all about. I seemed pleased because I was A1 and would be a soldier in no time at all.

The letter notifying me to report in the north-east of England arrived a week or so later. It gave me just three days' grace to say my farewells.

'They don't waste any time, do they?' Mam remarked.

'I suppose not,' I replied.

I noticed that there were no tears from Mam this time. I was glad at that, she had accepted the inevitable, although she looked sad.

The morning of departure came. What and where was I going to? Yes, my papers said report to so-and-so on the north-east coast of England, but what lay before me? It certainly wasn't a holiday, there was a war on, you know. These thoughts raced through my mind as I sat eating my breakfast. Poor Mam was busy getting my things to take with me. My mam, ever there when we needed her. I was going to miss her for sure.

I looked round my humble home, a home that had seen everything, laughter and sorrow, but at least it held a family together through good and bad. A place to run to for a jam butty when I was hungry, or a first-aid post when I fell and cut my knee. No matter how humble, it was my home and my family that I might never see again.

'Everything is ready for you, love,' Mam said, putting my sandwiches in a suitcase that had seen better days. 'I can't fasten this side. I think the lock is broken. I'll get a bit of string to tie round it,' she said as she tried to lock my case.

'Don't worry, Mam, it'll do. I'll manage with it like it is,' I replied.

'Well, make sure you don't lose anything,' Mam said as she put her coat on.

'Where do yer think you're going, Mam, at this time of morning?' I asked.

'To station with yer.'

'Oh no yer not. Yer staying right here. I'll say cheerio and just think I'm going to work. Where's Dad?' I said as I gave my hair a final comb.

'He's here now,' Mam replied. 'I can hear his clogs.'

And sure enough, there was Dad coming out of the gasworks gate. Same old dad, he had a lump of coal under his coat. Habits are hard to lose, I thought. Straight into the kitchen he went, got rid of the coal and said,

'Any tea Lizzie?'

'I've just poured you one. It's there on table.'

Dad picked it up, poured some in his saucer, blew on it and gulped it down.

'I'll have to go, Mam,' I said, 'or I'll miss train. It goes at seven-fifteen.'

I went to her, put my arms round her and gave her a hug. She was crying now all right, but I ignored it.

'Cheerio, Dad,' I said, holding out my hand which he grasped in a strong grip. This was his emotion, a hard grip. It showed me he cared.

'Good luck, son, and God bless,' he said as I searched his face for some sign of love, but no, he kept it beneath the surface somehow. His steel-grey eyes looked straight at me. I picked up my bag and without one word, I was off up the street until I came to the corner. Before I turned, I looked back and waved to Mam who was standing in the doorway.

When I got to the station, the train was at the platform. I got into an empty compartment. I wanted to be alone. That's how I felt as the train moved out. But one thing I did remember as we approached the bridge and that was to look out at the house where I had seen Kathleen, the girl I couldn't get out of my mind.

When I arrived in Manchester, I found the station full of people—sailors, airmen, soldiers, land army and civilians with suitcases and bags, but like me and the people in uniform, they were going to join their units. Red-capped soldiers were everywhere checking passes. An old man with an accordion was playing sentimental tunes like *We'll meet again* and *We're going to hang out the washing on the Siegfried Line*, songs that were meant to build up your morale. Somehow, I didn't feel lonely any more. I felt proud to be part of this scene that confronted me. I was going to be a soldier.

The letter that I had taken to the lovely Irish girl, Kathleen and the letter I had received from H.M. Government calling me to war were destined to change my whole future.

I boarded my train, getting into a now crowded compartment. Putting my broken bag where I could, I sat in the corner near the window. The platform was full of people. Wives were embracing husbands, mothers kissing their sons and daughters, sweethearts in fond embrace. I could see women holding on to their menfolk with children at their side, as the whistle blew for the train's departure, some men just making it on to the train as it moved out, the smoke from the engine enveloping the people momentarily. The man on the accordion quickly changed his tune to *Goodbye, goodbye, we wish you all the luck, goodbye*.

It didn't take long before everyone in the carriage was

talking. Stranger was talking to stranger, it didn't matter now; we were all in the same boat, so to speak—in this case, all on the same train.

As we reached our destination, we saw groups of soldiers on the platform. They were N.C.O.s waiting for us.

'Right, you lot,' one N.C.O. shouted in our carriage, 'grab your belongings and fall in here. Move now, we haven't all night.' (It was late afternoon when we arrived.)

The N.C.O. got us into some sort of order, then called our names from a sheet of paper he held in his hand. When he had finished he bawled out,

'Quiet, you're in the army now.'

We had been talking to each other, but now complete silence as a very smart little sergeant marched up.

'Report, corporal,' the sergeant bawled out.

'Present and correct, sergeant,' the corporal answered.

'Right, pay attention you lot, while I introduce myself. My name is Sergeant Davey. I don't want to know your names yet, I'll know soon enough to your sorrow, make no mistake. You belong to me now. I have to make soldiers of you bedraggled lot in six weeks, God help me.'

We laughed at his remark.

'Right, corporal, march them off.'

'Attention, right turn, quick march,' the corporal bawled.

What we looked like, I can't say. A group of lads from all walks of life carrying suitcases, going to be made into soldiers.

Chapter Five

RELEGATION

My life in the army began. The first two days were quite enjoyable, getting kitted out with everything a soldier needs. The uniforms were too big, the underwear too rough and the boots too hard.

Our beds were 'polyasses' (palliasses) filled with straw, placed on the floor in a regimental fashion; a hard tube-shaped object served as a pillow. The absence of pyjamas (which I never owned at home, anyhow) made it very uncomfortable indeed on bare legs, something we had to get used to.

Our training started in earnest on the third day. 'Reveille' at six o'clock, ablutions outside; it was winter and freezing cold and so was the water we washed and shaved with. Back in and change into P.T. kit and out again at the double for strenuous exercises that made you sweat and stiff all over. Dismissed. Back in at the double and change into uniform, grab your mess-tin, and parade for breakfast—one soya sausage and a burnt bit of bacon that looked lost on your tin plate, a thick piece of bread, and a ladle full of what they called tea. At least, that's more than I got during the depression, I thought. Then, it was a slice of bread and dripping. It was hard for the lads who had been used to better things at home, yet a bit of good came from it. They knew what it was going to be like to live rough.

There was no let-up at all from the lance-corporals to the sergeant-majors. You daren't look sideways at any of them. We were harassed and bullied, in drill, in weapon training, route marches and lectures. Some lads who couldn't stand the pace went absent; that was known as A.W.O.L. These were usually caught, given 28 days in a military prison, known in army terms as the 'glasshouse', a place, I believe, you didn't want to visit twice. From what I heard, they were fifty times worse than a civilian prison. Your hair was shaved off (they were the first known skin-heads). From the moment they entered the glasshouse gate, they did everything at the double, from going to the toilet to getting their meals. Some of the prison subordinates were sadistic.

I once entered one of these places as an escort, taking a prisoner in for punishment, and from the time we put our feet in the gate, which closed with a big metallic clatter, I was made to do double-time with my prisoner, at the same time answering the sergeant-major's questions.

'Up, up, up,' the sergeant-major kept shouting, till I thought I would drop.

'Escort, dismiss,' the sergeant bawled out. Believe me, I doubled to that gate in double quick time, and not until I heard it close behind me did I breathe a sigh of relief. I just leaned against those large iron gates and said, 'Thank Christ for that', at the same time wiping my brow. That was known as army discipline.

Days went by. Every day, no let-up. We got to know Sergeant Davey intimately. He called us bastards, he bullied, he made us drill and drill, he made us go over assault courses until we nearly dropped. But one thing was sure: from that bedraggled lot that came from the station with their suitcases, lads from all walks of life, shops, offices and what have you, only a few weeks before, were being turned out what was to be proved the finest infantry soldier in the world, the British 'Tommy'.

I had the shock of my life when our six weeks were up, our training complete. My name, with others, was called out to report to the company office. Some of my mates called out, 'Watch it Spud, you're in for the high jump', and began to rag

55

me. As I went to report, someone shouted, 'Maybe it's a stripe you're getting', and laughed.

'It might be at that, then you lot had better watch out,' I said jokingly.

But I soon knew why we were sent for. The sergeant-major was at his desk. Sergeant Davey stood rigidly at his side, a cane tucked under his armpit, when a corporal marched us in.

'The men you wanted, sir,' the corporal said crisply.

'Men!' the sergeant-major said, 'Men! I've shit 'em better.'

'Christ,' I said to myself, 'what's wrong?'

Then the sergeant-major started. He went on and on while we stood there like sheep, telling us our faults.

'And now you're bloody relegated. While all your mates are going on leave, you lot are staying here for a further three weeks' training. You're nothing but numbskulls. What are you?' he bawled out. There was silence.

'Say it,' he said.

'Numbskulls.'

'What?' he bawled out again.

'Sir,' we all shouted out loud.

'Take them out of my sight, Sergeant Davey, and I want a daily report on their progress. Do you hear?' the sergeant-major said.

'Sir!' the sergeant bawled. 'Attention. Right turn, double march, up, up, up', he kept on bawling until we got outside.

'Halt, you've heard the sergeant-major, you know what to expect. Right, dismiss.'

I was flabbergasted. I knew I wasn't good at explaining things like the Bren gun, but this to me was degrading. My mind went back, searching for the cause for all this. I know I blamed my school; I blamed my teachers, they didn't have time for my sort; I blamed the whole blasted system; but I never thought of blaming myself.

'I should start blaming myself, then I might get somewhere,'

56

I thought. I would teach myself, I would get books somehow, even if I pinched them from the company office. I knew the Catechism of the church and I could recite Mass in Latin. Why not do the same with weapons and drill, and manoeuvres and such, I thought.

'I'll show that lot,' I said to myself, 'you'll see.'

It was a very disappointed soldier who walked into the barrack-room to see my mates getting ready to go on leave. They couldn't believe it when I told them I had been relegated.

'You're going without me this time,' I said.

'Oh that's great,' a mate of mine called Jimmy said. 'We promised, me, you, Robin and Pat that we would stick together, no matter.'

'Well,' I replied, 'you've got them. Me, I'll be the lonely one until you get back.'

'We're not coming back here, Spud. We have to report to a camp in Northumberland.'

'How's that?' I said.

'Well, its only a training depot, this, and we have to make room for other intakes.'

That evening, I went out with Jimmy, Robin and Pat for a drink. I must admit I wasn't very good company, but I made the best of it. I said my farewells the next morning as the lads left for the station. I kept a brave face on. It was Saturday and I was detailed for guard duty for the weekend. It was going to be a dead place, so I didn't mind the duty. It also gave me the chance to 'nick' some pamphlets from the company office. When I wasn't outside with my rifle, I would sit on my bunk bed in the guardroom and read and read. I did this religiously for two weeks; in the evenings, not going out at all. When I had learned one thing, I was on to another. I became so proficient, I am sure I was as good as Sergeant Davey himself. Like my Catechism at Church, I knew a lot of these pamphlets off by heart.

57

The new intake had arrived and settled in. I and the other relegated lads had to start all over again. I felt big, training with raw recruits and I showed off a little. At the end of my third week, I was given my test by Sergeant Davey and an officer. They were both so surprised at my knowledge that the officer recommended me for potential N.C.O. This I got two weeks later and helped out as an N.C.O. for the remainder of the training. I felt on top of the world when the new lads called me 'corporal'.

As soon as these lads were trained, we moved farther up the coast to man defences, billeted in a large hotel on the sea front. I was in charge of a section of men, doing around-the-clock duty in a concrete pillbox, surrounded by barbed wire and minefields, an unwelcome task. The nights were long and dark; that was, until the German bombers came. That unmistakable drone could be heard long before they got to the coast. Then the sky lit up from the powerful beams of our searchlights, trying to guide our anti-aircraft guns on target. As the planes passed over the coast line, scores of them, the searchlight would pick up one in its beam, its metallic body glistening, and a cascade of tracer bullets would escalate upwards, trying to hit the target. Unfortunately, the planes were too high and out of range. Fighter planes of the Luftwaffe were higher still, guarding these monsters of destruction, until they reached their target. At this stage of the war, the Germans were defiant, daring our fighters to challenge them.

I would fire my Bren-gun at the bombers, knowing I could never hit them, but it made me feel better.

'They must be laughing their bloody heads off, those bastard Jerries, doing just what they want,' I said to my men. 'How the bloody hell are we going to beat them?'

The drone of the planes grew fainter as they went on their way inland, our guns went quiet and the searchlights went out, one by one. Everywhere along the coast went dark and quiet again, as searchlights and guns could be faintly seen and heard in the distance.

Night after night, depending on the weather, they came. I wondered at times, why we couldn't stop them. The truth was, with what? We hadn't been prepared for this war. We should have been, we had plenty of warnings from Nazi Germany, or I should say, the men at the top did, but they took no heed. The sins of our fathers were with us.

The next morning, after one such night on duty, I was relieved by another section of men. I marched our blokes back to H.Q. The little children, with their gas masks slung over their shoulders, were on their way to school. They would wave to us as we passed them, smiling all over their faces. I knew they looked to us as their protectors, we would beat those Germans for them. I could see it written on their faces. If only we could beat them. I thought, 'If only we could, for their sakes.'

As we went along the sea front, we saw the Home Guard on parade—middle-aged and old men, butchers, tailors, candle-stick makers, all doing their bit before they opened their shops for the day.

After I dismissed my men, I had to report to H.Q. with my report. I was in the corridor when I saw the sergeant-major.

'Ah, Murphy,' he said. 'Just the man I want to see. Come in my office a moment, will you?'

'Yes, sir,' I said, coming to attention, then followed him in.

'I'm afraid I've got some bad news for you, corporal,' he said.

My stomach gave a turn.

'It's not from home, is it, sir?'

'No, nothing like that,' he replied. 'Those lads you trained with. You had some pals amongst them, I believe.'

'Yes, sir,' I said, wondering what was coming next.

'You knew they were going overseas,' he said.

'Yes, sir, I heard they were.'

59

'Well, we have just had word. Their ship was torpedoed and sunk and all were lost.'

'God Almighty. No,' I shouted out. 'No. All of them dead?'

'As far as we know, yes. Some could have been picked up, but we can't bank on it. We could get word later that some were saved, possibly,' the sergeant-major went on. 'I'm sorry, corporal, to have to tell you this, but just think how lucky you and the other lads were when you got relegated.'

'Yes, sir, I suppose so,' I said dejectedly. 'I am lucky.' Poor old Jimmy, Robin and Pat. God help them, I muttered as I went to my billet. Poor sods.

I was on duty again tonight and I must get some sleep. I didn't want any breakfast. I just lay there on my kip, thinking of those lads that I had known so well.

After a few weeks on coastal defence, I was given a week's leave, something I had been looking forward to for quite a while. I couldn't contain myself as I got my pass and rail warrant from the company office. I was going home, my home. I had got some chocolate that I had saved for Mam, I had some thick twist for Dad and I had some presents for my young sisters and brother.

I remember it was around seven in the evening on a Friday. The house was empty when I arrived. I ran in the kitchen. I shouted upstairs. It was empty all right. A bright fire burned in the grate and that old black sooty kettle was steaming on the hob. I looked around. A nice cloth draped over that big-legged table with a vase of flowers in the middle. Everywhere looked good and clean.

I went back into the kitchen for a quick wash. The big brass tap on the lead pipe still hung loose from the wall.

'And you're still here,' I said, looking at the mangle and dolly tub. 'By gum, it's grand to be home.'

After I had washed and spruced up, I ran up to Mrs. Bennett's. She was quite old now, but still there, thank God.

She was sitting in her rocking chair when I went in.

'Hello, love,' I shouted. She was deaf and I didn't want to frighten her. 'It's me, Joe, I'm home on leave.' She looked round.

'Who is it?'

'It's Joe.'

'Ee, it's Joe,' she said. 'Come 'ere, love, let me look at you.'

I went round in front of her and knelt by her rocking chair on one knee and held her hand.

'I'm old now, Joe love, and I'm tired.' She was crying as she said it.

'You're not old to me, love,' I said kissing her on the cheek.

'Stand up, love, let's see you in yer uniform,' she said. I stood up and faced her.

'You do look smart,' she said. 'You're a soldier now, and it only seems like yesterday you toddled into my house.' She held out her frail hands for me to hold.

'You've still got Polly,' I said, looking at the parrot in the cage.

'I 'ave that,' she replied. 'It'll go when I go, I suppose.'

'Don't talk like that. You'll both be here when I come back from war and everything will be just the same as we left it, you'll see,' I replied. 'I'll have to go now. I haven't seen me mam and dad yet, but I'll see you tomorrow, please God.' She got up slowly from her rocking chair and walked over to her cupboard, getting a bottle and a small glass.

'Have this before you go, love,' she said, filling the glass. 'I've given you a glass of this since you were about seven years old.'

'Thanks,' I said as I took a sip. It was my favourite ginger wine. 'That was good,' I said, finishing it.

'Go on now and see your mam,' she said as she took the bottle of wine back to the cupboard.

'O.K., see you some time tomorrow. Goodnight and God bless.' I gave her a kiss.

'Goodnight, love,' she replied.

'It's our Joe,' Mam shouted as she got up from her chair, a big smile on her face.

'How's my little girl then?' I said as I put my arms round her and held her close.

'What a nice surprise,' Mam said. 'Why didn't you tell me you were coming home?'

'I wanted to surprise you,' I said.

'I'll get you a cup of tea. Are you hungry?' Mam said.

'No, not yet, but I'll have a bean mixture later on. Where's Dad?'

'He's in corner pub, I suppose.'

'Where's Hilda and Kathleen and young Brian?'

'They're out somewhere. I've been to pictures, first house. Ee, it was good. Ronald Coleman in "Prisoner of Wenda".'

'You mean Zenda, Mam, not Wenda,' I replied.

'That's right, its about this prince,' Mam said.

'I don't want to know, Mam, don't tell me. I'll probably want to see it myself,' I replied. 'Yer just the same as ever, Mam.'

She laughed.

'Here's yer cup of tea. Sit down and talk,' and that's just what we did for over an hour. I read letters from my brothers Tom, John, Frank and Jim, and we looked at photographs.

'Mam,' I said as I put a photograph down on the table, 'do you ever see Kathleen, the girl from t' doctor's?'

'I have seen her, a few times but not very often,' Mam replied. 'Don't tell me you still think of her, do you?'

'I do that, quite a lot,' I said. 'I only wish I could meet her.'

'Don't be daft. You know such a lot of girls,' Mam said.

'I do, but none like her, Mam,'

I jumped up from my chair.

'I'm going down to see Dad for half an hour, Mam, I won't be too long.'

'Do,' Mam said, 'he'll be pleased to see you.'

Dad was pleased to see me. He even ordered me a pint.

'I don't drink pints, Dad, just a gill.'

'Tha's a man now, lad, and if a son of mine takes a drink, then it's a pint. Give 'im a pint, George,' Dad said to the landlord, 'he's my son.'

'I thowt he might be, Jack, and he's a lance-corporal I see.'

'Ay,' Dad said proudly, so I noticed. 'When did'tha get that?' he said, turning to me.

'Oh, a couple of weeks ago.'

'Good, keep it up,' Dad replied.

I talked with Dad more than I had ever done in my life. I stayed with him until the pub closed and when we got home, we still talked. Mam got me my bean mixture and Dad had a fish for supper. I had missed my sisters and brother, they had gone to bed.

It was Dad who did all the talking, taking me through the First World War, reliving his experiences.

'He's had enough of that, Jack,' Mam said, 'let him go to bed. He must be tired.'

'Righto, Lizzie, we're coming now,' Dad would say, but still he talked and talked. I really didn't mind at all; I got to know more about my Dad then than ever I had. I could understand why he was like he was, quick-tempered and hard. So now, I dared to ask him why, something I would never have dared to do before the war.

'Well,' he said, 'I admit I was hard on yer all. It was a bit of a responsibility bringing eleven kids up, clothing and feedin' ye on just one wage. I had to make ye hard, it's a hard world. None of yer were ever in police hands, were yer? That was because you were frightened of me and knew what to expect if you did get into trouble.'

Eventually I managed to get to bed, tired and weary from our long talk.

'Give me a shout in the morning, Dad, when you're ready for work.'

'Right, Joe, lad, I'll do that.'

To my surprise, Mam was up and doing the next morning when I came downstairs. Dad had gone to work.

'I meant to light fire before you got up, love,' Mam said.

'Ay, Mam, we don't come down to a fire in th'army, you know. You get some breakfast for us both and I'll light fire.'

'Right, love, but don't forget to empty th'ashes out of th'eshole first, will yer?'

I hadn't heard that phrase for a long time but I knew that it meant I had to get the ashes out from under the grate.

The morning was going fast. I had been busy pressing my uniform and polishing my boots and brasses. I had nowhere important to go, I just wanted to go round the town and see the lads I knew, if they were still around.

I walked proudly up the main street, stopping at the butcher's, looking in the window. The shop was empty of customers, the butcher, Mr. Hooper, was busy cutting his meat. He hadn't noticed me at his window, so I walked in. His back was to me as he prepared the meat.

'Can I have a sheep's head for me dad's dinner, and will yer split it?' I said.

Mr. Hooper looked round.

'Well,' he said, 'if it isn't Joe Murphy. When are yer going back?' (That was always the question people seemed to ask.)

'I've only just come,' I said.

'That's what I meant,' Mr. Hooper said, 'how long 'ast got?'

'A week,' I replied. 'It's a long time since you towd me to get me grubby hands off yer counter, in't it, Mr. Hooper?'

'Ay, lad,' he said with a sigh, 'it's a long time. Now look at thee—a smart young fella fighting for his country. But I must say, yer might have been a bit grubby, but they were hard days, Joe, especially for large families like yours. Yer Mam and

Dad must be very proud of yer. How many are in th'army?'

'Five of us, Mr. Hooper,' I said, rather proudly.

'By gum, five of yer,' Mr. Hooper exclaimed, 'that's just great.'

Some customers came into the shop, so I said, 'I'll see you again, Mr. Hooper.'

'Call back before lunch, I'll have a bit of something for yer dinner,' Mr. Hooper replied.

'Right, I will. See you,' I shouted as I went out of the shop.

What happened next was to please me more than anything. I couldn't have planned it any better if I'd tried. Coming towards me, holding a little boy by the hand, was Kathleen. I just couldn't believe it, the girl I thought I would never see again. It was up to me now. I was shaking, I'm sure as I said, 'Hello, Kathleen.'

She looked at me, I suppose wondering who this soldier was.

'Do you remember me?'

Her face showed surprise.

'I think so,' she replied.

'You remember, I brought a letter to you once, that came to my house,' I said.

She put her hand to her mouth, as if in thought.

'I do for sure,' she replied in a soft Irish brogue, her lovely face wreathed in a smile that captivated me. I couldn't let her go this time, I thought, and without stopping to think, I said to her, 'Will you come dancing tonight with me?'

'I hardly know you,' she replied.

'Please come. Will you?' I said.

She hesitated to answer.

'Please,' I repeated. 'I'll look after you, I promise.'

Whether it was my pleading or that she felt sorry for me, I don't know, but suddenly she said, 'Alright, then, I will.'

'You will?' I said, as if I should have been surprised. 'Great, you don't know how long I've waited for this to happen. I just can't get over it. I— —'

'Where do I meet you?' she asked, interrupting me.

'Oh yes, will the Town Hall be alright? Say seven o'clock?'

'Seven o'clock. Yes, that will be alright,' she answered.

'You'll be there?' I asked.

'I'll be there,' she replied with a smile to melt my heart. 'I must go now, I'm late already.'

'Yes, yes,' I said. 'But don't forget, seven o'clock.'

I stood there and watched her until she turned the corner. I seemed rooted to where I stood. I don't think there was a happier man anywhere.

My mother was delighted—different to how she reacted when, a few years ago when I was sixteen, she saw me with a girl and chased me down the street with a broom that she had been sweeping the front step with. I couldn't believe it when she shouted at me, 'What are yer doin' with that girl?' 'Nothing, Mam,' I replied. Then she chased me. I just grabbed the girl's hand and ran. The girl, quite out of breath, wondered what was happening. In fact, that was the last time I saw her. I bet she thought we were mad.

That was a long time ago—things were different now.

I met Kathleen at seven o'clock. I had been waiting under the clock from quarter to seven. She, too, had been waiting, round by the hotel across the road, waiting and peeping round the corner to see if I had turned up first. When she saw me, she still waited until that clock struck seven o'clock.

We had a marvellous night together at a local dance hall, except for a few of the girls I knew who pestered me to dance with them. They just didn't understand, I only wanted to dance with Kathleen. I wanted her for my girl and I was frightened to dance with anyone else. I was wrong, I know, to ignore the girls I knew, even went to school with. They pestered me so much that Kathleen said,

'I'll go home now. You stay and dance with your friends.'

'Oh no you don't,' I said. 'I brought you and I'll take you

home. Get your coat, we'll go right now. I don't want any of these girls. They're nice, I know, and I know them well, but, Kathleen, I only want you. I really mean that, I love you.'

'I'll get my coat then,' she said, 'we'll go home together.' She went to the cloakroom.

'I'm sorry, Mary, Veronica,' I said to a couple of the girls, 'I don't mean to be rude to any of you, but I'm going with Kathleen. Goodnight.'

The girls didn't answer as I went to meet Kathleen at the door. I looked at her sad face.

'Are you sure you want to leave?' she asked.

'I've never been more sure,' I replied, putting my arm round her shoulder, as we walked out into the night.

That was the beginning of a long, turbulent and abstract love affair, lasting six years, and taking us farther and farther apart and placing me in untold dangers; from the shores of England to Africa, India, Afghanistan, Burma and Malaysia, seeing the horrors of war that were unbelievable, and trying to avoid diseases I had never heard of before like cholera, rabies, sleepy sickness, beriberi, smallpox—all this beside that brutal enemy, the Japanese soldier, known to us as the Nips.

My leave had been long over. I had been back with my unit for a few months, moving about the country doing manoeuvres. I was selected for a Physical Training Course at Catterick for three weeks. I passed this with honours and qualified to become a P.T. Instructor. I won my Crossed Swords badge and was promoted to full corporal.

Dunkirk, that terrible catastrophe had happened; this little island of our's was being bombed night and day. Thousands of people were getting killed and there was talk of invasion by the Germans. Our backs were to the wall, and we trained recruits as fast as they came in. My outlook was different now; I began to enjoy training these men to become soldiers, to learn new tactics and put over to them everything I

67

knew from the textbooks. I knew this was the only way we could beat the Germans, that is why I enjoyed it.

I wrote to Kathleen often, and she wrote to me. It didn't surprise me one bit when I heard I was on 'Embarkation Leave'. It was the summer of 1941. Having written to Kathleen, she met me at the station. This girl, who I had waited so long to meet, was now my girl, all mine.

'We will go home, Kathleen, and see my mam, then after I've had my tea and a wash, we'll go for a walk. Come on,' I said, holding her hand. 'I've only got ten days and I want every possible moment with you.'

She squeezed my hand.

After seeing my mam, I felt selfish leaving her so quickly, but she understood, I know. As I walked up the street with Kathleen, I said to her,

'Do you realize I won't see you for a very long time, maybe never?'

'Please, Joe, don't talk like that, it frightens me,' Kathleen said. 'We have a few days together. Let's enjoy them, and don't ever say anything like that again.'

'I just face facts, my love. There's a war on which we aren't even winning. Every day it's bad news,' I said, 'so what else can I think? I'm sorry if I've upset you. I'm no defeatist, I'll fight with the best and I'll give my best, that's for sure. I only hope it's worth it. When this lot's over, will the powers-to-be give me their best, I wonder?'

While I was muttering on, Kathleen had gone silent. We were still walking, holding hands. I looked at her, she was beautiful, something worth fighting for. I stopped and swung her into my arms, holding her tight. Her face was close to mine.

'Marry me, Kathleen, will you?'

'Marry you, you say? What do you think my mum would say? I would have to ask her permission,' Kathleen replied.

'Good God, how long would that take?' I asked. 'I've only got this week. Do you have to ask permission?'

'I'm afraid so,' Kathleen answered.

I still held her close.

'You're so, so innocent, Kathleen. That's one good reason why I love and respect you and I won't take advantage of you. I want you so very much, but I'll marry you first.'

'I'll marry you, Joe, when you return home. I'll wait for you no matter how long that is,' Kathleen said. 'That's a promise, cross my heart and hope to die.'

'Kathleen, you're just wonderful. Come on, I'll race you to that tree.'

I released her hand and let her run on first, keeping behind her.

'You beat me,' I said, as we got to the big oak tree in the field behind the cricket pitch. Kathy was out of breath as she sat down and leaned against its massive trunk.

'What a beautiful tree this is,' Kathleen said as she gazed up at its leafy branches. 'It's so big and strong.'

'It sure is big', I said, 'I'll tell you what. As I feel romantic, I'll make a little ditty up. We'll make this tree the symbol of our love. What do you say?'

Kathleen laughed.

'Let me hear it,' she said.

'Give me time to think, and don't you dare laugh at me.' I sat down beside her. 'Let me see now. Oh yes. Are you ready?'

Kathleen nodded.

'I'll come back pretty Kathleen, come back to thee,
Come back, where I belong,
For my love is as strong as this old oak tree,
I'll come back, sweet Kathleen, come back to thee.

Tomorrow I sail across the wide open sea,
To faraway lands I go.
Yet our love will be strong like this old oak tree,
Please wait, my Kathleen, please wait for me.

I'll return, sweet Kathleen, where'er I may be,
Return from fighting the foe.
Our love will last like this old oak tree,
It's the symbol of love for Kathleen and Joe.'

'You're crying,' I said, as I took her in my arms. 'You were laughing before; surely I'm not that good at poems. I just meant to— —'

'It was lovely', Kathleen said, interrupting me. 'It was really. I just couldn't help crying, I'm sorry.'

'Here, wipe your eyes,' I said, handing her my handkerchief. 'It's clean, my mam just gave it to me. Let's sit here for a while. I'll tell you what, Kathleen. You know my family, don't you? Well, you can tell me all about yours. I know you come from Ireland. I'm half Irish, you know. With a name like Murphy, I should be, and yours the same—what a coincidence. When's your birthday?'

'October,' Kathleen replied.

'When in October?' I asked.

'The thirtieth.'

'What?' I almost screamed it out. 'It's impossible.'

Kathleen looked dumbstruck.

'Why?' she asked.

'Because it's my birthday on the thirtieth of October. We are like twins. That's sealed it,' I said. 'We were made for each other without a doubt.'

We talked and talked under the tree until sunset. My first day of leave was coming to an end.

The days passed very quickly. Every minute of every hour of every day was divided between my family and my girl. I enjoyed it to the full. But now it was my last night at home. I had just left Kathleen and was sitting talking to Mam.

'I've packed your things, Joe,' Mam said, 'so make sure I haven't missed anything out. Just check, won't yer?'

'I will, Mam, but I'll just go and have a drink with Dad

70

for the last half-hour, and then I'll see to it. I want to go off tomorrow without any fuss, you know what I mean, Mam, no crying. It only makes me feel bad.'

'I can't help it if I do cry,' Mam said, 'it's not easy, you know.'

'Yes, Mam, see you later.'

Mam had my breakfast ready at five-thirty a.m. My train left at six o'clock, the first train out, and it was but ten minutes walk to the station. Dad was in bed, so my farewell was short and quick, but, man that he was, he kissed me—that gesture I never forgot.

The hardest part was Mam. This parting of her soldier sons came too often, six in all before the war ended—some woman, was my little Mam. That corner where I last waved as she stood on the doorstep, must have been like a monument to her, for this was the spot where each son had waved his farewell, the corner where I looked back with tears.

Chapter Six

A LONG JOURNEY

As I boarded my train, I knew I had one more thing to do, one very important thing.

I had agreed with Kathleen the night before, that she mustn't come to the station, but to be at a certain window, overlooking the bridge which the train passed over at six-five a.m. on the dot. As the train approached the bridge, my heart thumped loudly in my chest. I was leaning out of the window. I could see her in her night attire, framed in that large window. With my cap in my hand, I started to wave frantically. She saw me and she waved too. I stretched out my hand, trying to touch her, she was so close.

'Kathleen,' I shouted, not caring for anyone, 'I'll come back, I'll come back, wait for me.'

She couldn't hear me, I know, but I still shouted as the moving train took me farther and farther away. I couldn't see her now, but I still waved, until it was no use waving any more.

I slumped into my seat in the corner and closed my eyes.

I had the main line train to get at Manchester. It was very full when I got on, but I soon found a seat and conversation with other military men. No one was a stranger, in uniform or out, and loved ones back home were momentarily forgotten. I was a soldier again and looking to the task ahead. My love would be abstract and confined to letter-writing, something a soldier got so used to doing.

I ran slap bang into a bad air raid on London, so I was

confined to the underground for quite a while. The London people were used to this. It didn't worry them too much—there was laughter and singing and plenty of cups of tea being shared round.

After the 'All Clear', I was on my way for the train to Dover. I got chatting to a couple of lads going to the same unit. Everything was peaceful until we got to Dover, then, as we left the station the shelling started, falling here, there and everywhere.

'Christ,' I said to one of the lads, 'it's like running the bloody gauntlet. Let's get to the camp quick.'

'Which way is it?' one of the lads asked.

'We'll ask that warden,' I replied.

The warden soon put us on the right track.

'Buses aren't running just now. You'll have to hump it, I'm afraid,' he said.

So we did, up a long steep hill, a couple of miles away. Eventually we arrived, tired, but in one piece and very, very thankful.

After reporting in at Battalion H.Q. office, we had to report to Company H.Q.s, then get settled into a barracks. It was getting late, I was hungry and tired.

'Where's the Naafi?' I asked one of the soldiers in the barrack room.

'I'll show when you're ready, but you'd better hurry,' he said, 'they close at nine-thirty and it's nearly nine o'clock now.'

'I'm ready,' I said, 'let's go.'

We were lucky, we managed to get eggs and chips—I did say 'lucky'. I had half my supper eaten, so had the other lads, when we heard the bloody dive-bombers getting louder and louder, then the siren went.

'Christ', I shouted, 'run. I mean, get down quick.'

Everybody in the room was on the floor when the first explosion came, somewhere outside. Then I heard shouting, 'Get to the shelters.' We all made one mad rush. I didn't know where the shelters were, I just went with the crowd. I was flat on the floor twice before I did reach the shelter. Quite a few dive-bombers were attacking the camp; the noise of these planes as they came diving in was really frightening—then the bombs.

'We'll be blown to rotten bits,' I said as I fell down the steps of the shelter. It was pitch black, you couldn't see anyone, only hear voices.

'Fucking hell, we're like rats in a trap down here, I'm going out. There's no bloody air,' I heard someone shout.

'Keep quiet,' I said, 'whoever's shouting. No one goes outside, that's an order, so just keep calm.'

I was shitting myself, but as a corporal, I had to keep discipline. The 'All Clear' sounded after about twenty minutes. It was a great relief to get out of that rat-hole they called a shelter.

That was a fine start on the first night with this unit. A fortnight and a few air raids later, I was at Southampton, aboard one of the ships in a large convoy, bound for India. To my surprise, I'd met a lad I had trained with up in the north-east, called Len Taylor.

'It's great to see you, Len,' I said. 'How did I miss you at camp?'

'Easy,' he said, with a laugh, 'I was late back off leave.'

'Christ, what did you get for that?' I asked.

'I came back on my own so the C.O. said I'd be charged on the boat,' Len replied.

'Well, there's one thing sure, Len, they can't confine you to barracks,' I said with a laugh.

It was bedlam on the ship. We were down in the hold, or it seemed like it, the portholes were near water level.

'It's crowded in here, Len; just look at those hammocks. We won't survive if we get hit, I'm sure. So this is where we eat, sleep and be merry,' I said. 'Talk about sardines.'

'What'll it be like in tropical waters?' Len said.

'With all those sweaty bodies and sweaty feet,' I added.

'Who's the corporal for this mess deck?' a sergeant called out.

'I am, sergeant,' I said.

'Right, report to the company office for your orders on "C" deck,' he shouted, 'and be quick.'

After I returned with my orders, it wasn't long before organization existed. I was kept busy making out rosters for this and that, getting to know alleys and gangways, who did so-and-so, everything that mattered in the smooth running of a troopship. This mess deck was my responsibility; it was our barrack room for how long? No one could answer that, and I had to answer to my sergeant for everything, so I didn't let up with the men until everyone was conversant with the routine—everything must go like clockwork.

There were a good few laughs that night as the men got into their hammocks, or I should say, tried to get into them. Some got in at one side and fell out of the other, but we did get the hang of it after a few unsuccessful attempts.

It was quite late. I lay awake thinking. It was quiet except for the snoring of a few of the men, and the occasional creak from the timbers of the ship.

'Are you awake, corp?'

It was Len in the next hammock.

'I am,' I replied.

'I think we're moving,' he said. 'Listen, I can hear the engines.'

My hammock began to sway.

'You're right, Len,' I said, 'we're off.'

'Have you got a girl, corp?'

'I have,' I said, 'she's called Kathleen.'

'I'm married,' Len said. 'I had to, she was pregnant.'

'You lucky sod, Len, I wish I could have got married,' I said. 'You don't know how lucky you are. You'll have a wife and kid to go back to.'

I talked on about Kathleen and the things we would do.

'Are you listening, Len?' but I got no answer. Len was fast asleep. I closed my eyes, hoping to sleep too.

I was awakened suddenly by the Orderly Sergeant and his witty remarks. It was 'Reveille'.

'Wakey, wakey then, you landlubbers, yer all at sea,' he called. 'Draw yer water skis, we're going on a route march.'

Men started to fall out of their hammocks galore. It was as bad as getting in them the night before.

That first day at sea we were busy getting our so-called organization organized—boat drill, action stations, and what have you, was a must.

I, as P.T. Instructor, was kept quite busy, and after a couple of days, we took it all in our stride and we found we had plenty of free time for relaxing and playing 'housy, housy', crown and anchor, and boxing, etc. We got a few interruptions from U-boat scares, but nothing serious.

One day, whilst on deck, I noticed for the first time that we had some nurses on board, which surprised me. They were confined to a certain deck and allowed to mix with the officers on 'A' Deck only, well out of reach of the soldiers. Envious eyes watched them at play.

'Lucky sods, these officers', you could hear someone say. I couldn't care less, they didn't worry me as Kathleen was fresh in my thoughts; thinking of her and writing to her was my satisfaction.

The ship sailed on as days and weeks slipped slowly by.

We were now in tropical waters. Whenever possible I would spend my evenings on deck. Finding a secluded spot, a hard thing to do, I would sit and write. Sometimes I would stand at the ship's rail, looking out at the multitude of ships in our convoy, conveying their human cargo. Destroyers of the Royal Navy darting here and there like sheepdogs guarding their flock, keeping a look-out for German or Japanese submarines, an unthankful task in this vast ocean.

I would gaze at the beautifully coloured flying fish as they left the water and skimmed for hundreds of yards, before falling back into the sea, only to reappear again, farther along. And the dolphins, always a pleasure to watch, leaping so high out of the water, they seemed to be following the ships for miles.

There was plenty of discipline on a troopship—there had to be, for danger stalked us night and day, as we zigzagged our way to our destination. This was always in the forefront of my mind, more so at night as I lay in my hammock. It was so hot down on our mess deck, so low down in the ship, that I would invariably get up on deck to sleep.

It was a grand feeling when we arrived at Cape Town and got shore leave. I couldn't get off the ship quick enough and on to terra firma. As I went down the gangplank with a couple of pals, Len and Jock, we saw and heard the 'Woman in White' singing for the troops. It was said that she met every troopship this way all through the war.

We hadn't walked fifty yards when a gentleman with a lady by his side, hailed us from an open car, parked near the dock gate.

'Excuse me,' the man called out, 'we would like to show you Cape Town and then have dinner at our residence.'

There were numerous people in cars taking troops as a sort of contribution to the war effort. Apparently, this was a practice they had adopted. As troopships arrived at this South African port, knowing where the troops were bound, they intended giving them a day to remember.

After conferring with Len and Jock, we agreed we would go.

'Thank you, sir,' I said, 'we accept your kind offer.'

The lady smiled as the man introduced himself.

'My name is Mr. Fitzpatrick, and this is my wife,' the man said, holding out his hand.

'Pleased to meet you, sir, madam. This is Len and this is Jock and I'm Joe,' I said.

'Right, lads, in you get, we're wasting time', the man said. 'You've a lot to see, a lot to eat and a lot to drink.' We got into the back seat and off we went, to spend a day we would remember for a long time. It was three very happy soldiers that drove back to the ship that night.

We had left Cape Town far behind and were days out in the Indian Ocean. It was quite late one night and so hot that I couldn't sleep. I was standing at the ship's rail, deep in thought, just watching the illuminated foam from the waves, as the ship cut its way through the water. It was very quiet, as the men who were on deck slept. I thought I was hearing things when I heard a voice say 'Hello'. It was a female voice, I thought. I looked round and saw that it *was* a female.

'I couldn't sleep,' she said as she stood at the rail beside me. 'It's too hot.'

'It'll be much hotter for both of us if you're caught here with me,' I said, looking round to see if anyone else had seen her. 'You're a nurse, aren't you?' I asked nervously.

'That's right,' she replied, 'a sister really, and I've got a headache, too much to drink really, I suppose. Have you a cigarette?'

'Sorry,' I said, 'no smoking on deck, rules you know. Come on, as much as I would love to talk to you, you must go back or we will both be in trouble. What deck are you on?'

' "C" deck,' she replied.

'Well, let's get you there quick,' I said, taking her by her arm.

'Kiss me goodnight,' she said, stopping and looking at me. 'Don't be scared, soldier, kiss me.'

Then, one of the soldiers lying near by shouted,

'For Christ's sake kiss her and let's get some sleep.'

I couldn't believe it. He must have seen us and thought I was an officer.

'I'll go when you've kissed me,' she said.

78

I didn't hesitate. I gave her a good kiss, and enjoyed it.

'Now will you go?' I said.

'I'll go,' she replied. 'Goodnight and thanks a lot. You're very nice and sweet.'

'Goodnight, nurse,' I said as I pushed open the door, leading to her quarters.

'Goodnight,' she said, putting her hand on my cheek. As the door closed to, I just said to myself, 'Thank God for that. Phew.'

The ship sailed on. Days and weeks passed and we were nearing our destination, but I never saw the nurse again, even when I saw them up on 'A' deck, I couldn't recognize her at all. Len and Jock didn't believe me when I told them what had happened. All I got was, remarks like, 'I'd have had her alright, in one of the lifeboats, what?', 'The bloody thought of it's given me the horn.'

'You're all bloody talk and you know it,' I said. 'What if I had tried anything and she screamed, do you realize what that would mean?'

Now I know I did the best thing.

One week after this incident, we were on deck as the ship anchored at Bombay. We were here at last. It had taken nearly thirteen weeks to get here. We must have been changing course scores of times. Thirteen weeks was a long time to be on a troop ship.

After we disembarked, we were taken to that camp, where every soldier arriving in India went, just a few hours from Bombay, a place known as Deulali—a place every soldier loves to leave. It was known, all right, for if any soldier, N.C.O. or officer did anything stupid, you would hear the remark, 'Oh him, he's "Doolali Tap".' Staying there long made you stupid.

I was glad, after I had been here a couple of days, to hear our stay wouldn't be too long, but it was made longer when we all got confined to camp. Bubonic plague was heard to have broken out in Bombay and up to Nazik Bazaar, a village near our camp. I had heard about this disease during lectures on the boat. We knew which diseases existed in India, and this was our first taste of it—a malady carried by rats that infected humans and was fatal. I never saw anyone with this infection, but what I heard about it was enough, and I was content to stay in camp even when the ban was lifted.

I also learned something about India and her people, from a lecture I attended. I was very interested and wanted to know of this intriguing country, her people and religions, at that time over fifty per cent of the population were Hindu and forty-five per cent Moslem; the remainder being the Sikhs, Christians, Buddhists, Parsees and Jews, each with their own ways and customs.

After we left Deulali we went to Delhi for a spell. Here it was soldiering at its best, getting into shape as a battalion of soldiers should be, plenty of hard discipline, brass cleaning and blanco—what is termed in the army as 'bullshit'. Parades and lectures were non-stop.

I, as a P.T. Instructor, was kept busy getting the men fit for our next move. We all thought it would be Burma—that was where the fighting was going on—but we were mistaken.

At last, after a couple of months, we were moving out.

Chapter Seven

NORTH-WEST FRONTIER

It was a smart and well-disciplined force that left Delhi for the North-West Frontier, a little disappointed, as we thought we would be going to Burma. It was all part of a scheme before we entered Burma. What better training ground could there be than the Frontier?

It was in this wild and desolate place that we got our baptism of fire; knowing what it was like to be shot at by the enemy. Some of my mates never knew because here, they died. When you heard the bullet, you were all right; when you didn't hear it, you were dead.

Peshawar, the last stopping place before the frontier. From here, we moved up to our base camp in convoy, along dusty narrow roads right into the foothills below the Himalayas, a vast range of mountains that seemed to touch the sky, a range of mountains that divided India from China and Russia, a great natural barrier.

I gazed in wonder at this mountainous country as we drove into our primitive camp of tents and bamboo 'bashas'. A loose-stoned wall surrounded the camp and was topped with 'dannet' wire. Soldiers on duty were constantly patrolling this wall, known as the perimeter, to prevent any of the tribesmen getting in, which they did from time to time. They were past masters at this art. As silent as a snake and as cunning as a fox, they could worm their way in somehow. It wasn't to murder or cause havoc, but to steal your rifle, ammunition, blankets, etc. That is why every soldier in camp had his rifle chained and attached to his wrist even when he slept. Then we had to take out the bolt and lock it in our kit box that we kept under the 'charpoy' (bed).

These tribesmen, it was said, could take a soldier's blanket from under him as he slept, by just using a feather. They would tickle you in your sleep, you would roll over then back again without wakening.

The latrines were situated outside the perimeter wall, with 'dannet' barbed wire behind them for protection. If you wanted to use the latrine at night, you had to take someone with you to stand guard while you had a 'shit'. Otherwise, you could have lost your testicles as the tribesmen did this if you weren't protected.

Our job on the frontier wasn't to fight the tribesmen, but to protect the convoys that passed through into China. We called this duty 'R.O.D.s'—road opening days. From leaving the camp, everything was done at the double, to get to our position where we could survey the roads and give protective fire if necessary. If we hadn't run, we would have been too easy a target for the tribesmen, who were always in position in the high rocky slopes. They would wait in these positions for days, to snipe at the soldiers as they left camp and took up their positions. The bullets would make a peculiar sound as they whizzed by. The reason for this was that they were 'dum-dum' bullets—the tribesmen would cut the nose off the 303, making it flat, causing a terrible mess when one hit you, and nine times out of ten being fatal.

I had returned to camp after my first venture of R.O.D., when I met Lieutenant Fox, an officer I had come out with from England, a young and friendly officer, with whom I had got on well. I saluted him as he approached.

'How are you, sergeant?' he asked with a smile. I didn't catch on for a minute. Then I said, 'Fine, sir, but didn't you say Sergeant?'

He replied, 'That's what company orders say, sergeant. I've

just read it. Congratulations.'

'Thank you, sir.'

Lieutenant Fox gave me a sly wink. A smile showed behind that big moustache that covered his upper lip.

'See you tonight,' he said as he walked off. I saluted him and ran to see the notice board at company H.Q. Yes, there it was in bold letters. I was a Sergeant with effect from today. I immediately went to my tent—I had to get my stripes on my uniform. I couldn't see the Indian boy who did a few jobs for me, so I got my shirts and took them myself to the company tailor.

'Stripes, Abdul,' I said to the Indian tailor. 'Sergeanti', putting three fingers across my forearm. 'Peechy—abhi.'

'Teeki, sahib,' Abdul said, counting my shirts. 'one hour sergeant sahib, Teeki.'

'Teeki, Abdul,' I said as I went away.

That evening, I was received into the Sergeants' Mess by Sergeant Bell, an old regular soldier who was acting Company Sergeant-Major.

'Sergeant Murphy, sir,' Bell said to the Regimental Sergeant-Major. 'A new member to our Mess, sir.'

'Pleased to have you, Murphy,' the R.S.M. said. 'Get the drinks in then. What are you waiting for?'

'Drinks? Who for?' I whispered to Sergeant Bell.

'The whole lot of us,' he said, and laughed. I didn't

As we sat having dinner, Sergeant Jones said to me, 'We have a sergeant missing, you know, Sergeant Palmers. He went absent last night.'

'What? You mean he's done a bunk?' I said.

'No, I don't think so. More likely he's been pissing about in the foothills, looking for a 'bint' (an Indian woman). He was was bibulous, always at the bottle! He'd drink whisky out of a sweaty sock, would Palmer,' Sergeant Bell said. 'And if he's gone out there, God help him.'

Before we had finished dinner, there was a clatter of bullets hitting the corrugated roof of the Mess. I jumped up from the table.

'What's that?' I asked.

'Sit down, lad,' the R.S.M. said. 'They're just letting us know that they're around.'

'Who's they, sir?' I asked.

'The bloody Pathans, of course,' the R.S.M. replied. 'You'll get used to it before you've been here long.

Two days later it was decided to send a patrol of Gurkhas out to try and locate Sergeant Palmers. If anyone could find him, the Gurkha soldier would. I was guard commander the night the Gurkha officer and his men left on their mission. I was sitting in the guardroom and had just finished writing a couple of letters home. One was for Kathleen, the letter I wrote religiously every night. Sergeant Jones walked in for a chat.

'I'm worried about Palmers, Spud,' he said. 'I think those bastards out there have got him, you know.' I listened intently as he talked. I was learning something about this frontier.

'I'll bet my bottom dollar he was looking for a stinking woman. Some bleeding hope of finding one here in this god-forsaken hole,' he said. 'There's plenty of sheep around. Why didn't he content himself with one of them?'

'What do you mean?' I said. 'Do you mean blokes would go with a sheep?'

'I'm bloody sure they would when they get hard up,' Sergeant Jones replied. 'It has been known, you know.'

'They must be hard up if anyone would do that. It's bloody disgusting,' I said. 'Fuck off, Jones, and tell that tale to the marines. I've heard it all now.'

I knew Jones had a few drinks down him, that's why he was talking like that, I thought.

'I'm off now then, Spud. I know you think I'm romancing, but you'll learn. Some of the old soldiers would shag a snake if it stopped wriggling.'

'I've heard it all, Jones. Goodnight,' I said.

'O.K. Spud, Goodnight,' Sergeant Jones replied, laughing as he went out.

'You hear some right old soldier's tales,' I said, turning to my corporal, 'but that takes the bun.'

'But I've heard about that before, sergeant,' the corporal said.

'Don't you start,' I said. 'I've heard about enough for one night. Go and check the guards.'

'Right, sergeant' the corporal said, as he slung his rifle over his shoulder and went out of the guardroom.

It was about 0930 hours the next morning when the Gurkha patrol got back to camp. Here they were, coming in the gate, with two Gurkhas carrying a stretcher of sorts. They stopped at the guardroom.

'Bad news?' I said to the Gurkha officer and looking over at the stretcher.

'Bad news Sergeant,' he replied, 'Sergeant Palmers is dead.'

'Corporal,' I shouted, 'get the duty officer, quick.'

The corporal ran off to Company H.Q. I stood near the covered body of Sergeant Palmers with the Gurkha officer. It wasn't long before the corporal was back with the duty officer —it was Captain Holmes.

I saluted as he approached. He went straight to the stretcher and grasping the cover, pulled it down, revealing Palmer's face. I looked as the officer said, 'The filthy swines.'

What I saw made me want to vomit. It was the ghastliest sight. I turned my head away. The officer seemed in a daze as he held the cover in his clenched fist. Then suddenly, he threw the cover back over the body.

'Take him away,' he shouted to the Gurkha officer. 'The tent next to the M.O.'s will do. Leave a guard with him and make your report.'

The Gurkha officer saluted and said, 'Right away sir.'

I turned and went into the guardroom as the body was taken away. He had been terribly mutilated. The most hideous thing I ever want to see. Captain Holmes followed me in, looking very concerned.

'Not a word about this, Sergeant, to anyone. I know it will get out, sometimes these things do,' he said, 'but the least said just now, the better.'

'Right, sir,' I replied and Captain Holmes went away to deal with the situation.

I couldn't eat properly at all that day and Sergeant Palmers' death was the chief topic. When asked what I saw, I just ignored the question or just said that I had seen nothing because his body was covered. Sergeant Palmers was buried at 1400 hours just outside the perimeter wall.

Day in and day out we soldiered, plenty of bull, guard duties, parades, lectures and R.O.D.s. I was just twenty-one years of age and a sergeant, and I was beginning to enjoy life on the frontier. It was much cooler here than on the plains of India, and with being a P.T. Instructor, I was fit, very fit.

I would run around those foot hills like a young antelope. It never occurred to me that I could be shot dead at any time when we were out of camp, taking up positions to guard our convoys through, for on a few occasions some lads did not get back to camp alive.

We were never allowed to forget where our final destination was to be after our duty here in Afghanistan—that place was Burma.

I was going on my round of duties one evening as 'orderly sergeant', when I heard a scream. It came from one of the Indian followers, he was hopping about on one foot and holding the other in his hand. The bundle he had been carrying was on the floor. I went over to him and, seeing who it was, I said, 'What's wrong, Ahmed?'

86

'Snake, Sahib, snake.'

I looked round. There it was, ready to strike again, the smallest snake I had ever seen, only about one foot long, its mouth wide open. I put the heel of my boot on its head and crushed it, then rushed to Ahmed who by now, had fallen down and was having convulsions. I drew the knife that I carried and caught hold of his foot, but I couldn't for the life of me see where the snake had bitten him. I broke out in a sweat as I tried to locate the tell-tale mark. Ahmed gave another convulsive shudder and lay still. A soldier near at hand shouted, 'I'll get the M.O., sarge.'

'Do,' I replied, 'tell him what's happened. Hurry,' I shouted as I knelt by the old Indian. 'I'm sure he's dead,' I said to myself. I looked at the dead snake. 'You're the queerest snake I've ever seen,' I said. I looked up, 'Where's that bloody M.O.?' I was talking to myself. The soldier came running back with the M.I. sergeant.

'It's you, Taffy,' I said to the sergeant. 'What do you make of this lot? That's what's done the damage,' I said, pointing at the snake. Taffy took one look at the dead snake and said, 'Crate, one of the deadliest.'

He put his ear to the Indian's chest, then shook his head.

'He's a gonner, I'm afraid, he'd have no chance. I'll see to his removal right away.'

'That snake, Taffy, a "crate" you say it is?' I said.

'That's right,' Taff answered, 'It's nicknamed the "bootlace" snake, because that's what it looks like on the floor, and if it bites you, it's curtains for you in a few minutes. It's deadly.'

'I'll remember that,' I said. 'You're going to see to old Ahmed then? I'll make a report at Company H.Q. O.K.?'

'Right, Spud,' Taffy said as I walked away. 'By the way, Spud, don't blame yourself in any way. There's nothing you could have done to save him.'

'That's a relief, Taff. Thanks,' I replied, looking at poor old Ahmed.

A few days later, I was on my way to Peshawar on a duty
It was a pleasant break from camp. I sat by the driver in a
fifteen-cwt vehicle. My rifle lay across my knees, ready for
any trouble. We certainly put a spurt on down the bare,
winding road, so as to be less of a target, and leaving a cloud
of red dust behind us.

'I bet those bastards have their beady eyes on us, sarge,
don't you think?'

'Of course they have, but they won't bother us. They're
too far away, and anyhow, we're in the open here,' I said.
'Just keep this speed up, we'll be O.K.'

I relaxed and settled back in my seat. After I had done what
I had to do in Peshawar, I told the driver that we'd have a
couple of hours in the bazaar, a safe enough place in daylight
for a couple of British soldiers and a place full of intrigue.

We saw the Pathan tribesmen strolling through the bazaar
with impunity. Tall, masculine men with rifles slung on their
shoulders and a couple of bandoliers criss-crossed over their
chest; their jet-black hair as shiny as a raven's, fell below their
turbans. Just going about their business, and not taking the
slightest notice of us, their arch-enemy—not here today, but
tomorrow, back in those foothills, they would do their best to
cut our throats.

'Boots, sahib, good boots for soldiers, sahib,' an Indian
called out, trying to sell his wares. I was interested, it might
be very primitive, but these Indian 'wallah's' were masters at
their art. I picked up a pair of boots and said, 'Kitne dam hai?'
(meaning, 'How much?').

'Very cheap for soldier, sahib,' the Indian repeated. I
looked at him. I knew I would only offer half of what he asked.

'Thus rupee,' I said (meaning 'ten rupee').

'Twenty rupee, sahib, very cheap.'

'Ten rupee,' I said.

'No, sahib, me poor man. Six chicos,' he replied, saying that
he had six children.

'Come on, Brett,' I said to the driver and began to walk away. I walked slowly, expecting the Indian to call after me. He did.

'Sahib,' he called. I stopped and looked back. He was holding the boots at arm's length.

'Ten rupee, sahib,' and I repeated the amount and paid him.

Farther along, we watched with fascination a fight between a king cobra snake and a little brave mongoose. The cobra standing, poised to strike, looked enormously tall, its hooded head swaying. The mongoose just sat a few feet away, its little eyes fixed firmly on the snake, not making a movement. Minutes ticked by, then without warning, the cobra struck like lightning. It missed. Just a slight movement from the mongoose made sure of that. Time after time, the cobra struck, until it began to slow up—it was tiring itself out. That was fine strategy from the mongoose, that's just what he wanted; then, when the right time came, the mongoose made its move. The cobra struck out for the last time. As soon as it hit the floor, the mongoose was round and gripping the snake's neck in a vice-like grip of its jaws. Over and over they rolled, sending the dust flying, the cobra twisting and turning, trying to shake off its adversary, but with no effect. That great little mongoose held on, biting deeper and deeper until Mr. King Cobra lay still and dead.

'That's great,' I said to Brett. 'I've always wanted to see that. I've heard about it and now I've seen it. What do you say to a pint?'

'Fine, if we can get one.'

We found some beer right there in the bazaar, in a seedy little restaurant, filled with turban-headed Indians, smoking from pipes attached to containers half-filled with water. They took long draws on these pipes held in clenched fists, until their cheeks sunk right in.

We stood watching them, when an Indian, probably the owner asked, 'Beer, sahib? Cold beer? We got, sahib. Sit down,' he said, pulling a chair out.

'Is it bottled?' I asked.

'Yes, sahib, bottled, only good stuff.'

He went off, returning with two large bottles of beer and two glasses. I paid him and, ignoring the glass, drank straight from the bottle.

'Not bad,' Brett said, 'but I'll bet it's been lifted.'

'Could be at that, but it's good,' I said, taking another gulp.

After the beer, we were on our way back to camp.

'I'm glad I got those boots, Brett. They were a real bargain.' I felt pleased with myself as I settled down in my seat for the long ride back.

A couple of months after my visit to Peshawar and a lot of soldiering in between, I was on detail with a couple of sergeants and an officer, together with fifteen men, two armoured cars and five fifteen cwt trucks. We had to go to Razmak, a military compound about twenty miles or so north of our base camp. This was to collect personnel who were being discharged from hospital, soldiers who had been wounded and sick. Quite a formidable force, I thought, just to bring a few blokes back to camp. I was to learn a big lesson from this venture; in fact, I was lucky to get back alive. Some of the lads never made it.

Our journey there was one of apprehension. The sun was big in a clear blue sky as our convoy wended its way up the dusty roads, through mountainous and rock-strewn country. Flashes of light could be seen as we climbed higher and higher, probably the tribesmen signalling our presence.

Seeing the flashes didn't worry us unduly—we were well equipped for any eventuality and we felt quite safe as we sped along. We got a good view of our camp far below on the plains. It looked so small and unimportant from this height. We reached Razmak, a well-guarded compound protected by a high solid stone wall, like a fortress, a distance of about twenty miles from our camp. Our stay there was short, only about two or three hours duration; a meal had been arranged for us before our return.

'That wasn't a bad run, was it, Ding-Dong?' I said to Sergeant Bell.

'No, but keep your bloody eyes peeled going back,' he replied. 'You saw their signals when we were coming up?'

'That's what they were then,' I said.

'That's just what they were, Spud, my boy, so take my word, don't relax.'

'Knowing you, Ding-Dong, I'll take your advice. Thanks,' I said.

We drove out of the gate at Razmak with twenty more men, unarmed, the discharge from hospital. We had gone about fifteen or sixteen miles and were in view of our camp in the distance below when it happened. It was on a notorious sharp bend. My leading truck was about fifty yards behind the armoured car, when a string of camels, led by a Pathan, came across our front, cutting us off from the armoured car which had turned the bend. I looked back quickly and saw that the trailer armoured car was out of sight too. It hadn't turned the bend, for as we stopped, the other trucks had to stop, leaving them vulnerable. On our right was a steep boulder-strewn slope, and on our left there was a forty-five-degree slope to the road below. I grasped the situation in a second.

'Drive on, you bloody idiot,' I shouted to the driver.

'But the camels,' he said.

'Ram 'em, ram 'em.'

The driver revved up and did just that. The squeals from those camels was terrible, but he kept ramming. The beasts went in all directions, as the firing started, bullets ripping through the canvas of the truck, killing some of our lads.

'Jump out,' I shouted. 'Get behind the trucks and take cover.'

It was hell let loose. Blood spurted everywhere as the lads got it. The noise was deafening. Whether they heard me or not in this din, I don't know. My driver was dead or unconscious at the wheel. I got out and shouted again.

'Get down here quick.'

The firing was constant, as some of the lads made it out and got to my side, shielded by the truck.

'Keep down and don't move,' I said. 'You can't be hit here.'

I then tried to see inside my truck but it was impossible. The bullets were ripping the canvas to shreds. I looked up and saw one lad just going to jump out, his hand and one foot on the tailboard, when he was hit, right through his throat. His body toppled out and jerked a few times.

'God Almighty, help us, please help us,' I pleaded. I was sweating profusely as I crouched at the side of that rear wheel. To make things worse, the bright sun was in our eyes and as I tried to get into a position to fire, I couldn't see a damn thing. The firing stopped. I looked along the road. It was the same story. What had happened to us had happened to them too. We were certainly trapped. The firing started again.

'Just keep down, lads. Don't move. We're safe here for a while.'

The firing had been heard at the camp, 'I'm sure they'll get us out of this mess.' I was talking to keep the lads' morale up—and my own. My thoughts were working overtime: my family, my Kathleen, all came into my head as my sweat mingled with my tears. God, if only we could fight back, I wouldn't mind.

'Look, sarge, someone's coming up the road, I think,' one of the lads said.

'What's he trying to do?' I said as we saw him stumbling from truck to truck. 'It's Captain Holmes,' I shouted as he nearly fell on top of me. He was bleeding and looked all in.

'If I can get to that armoured car, we can get out of this mess, sergeant,' he said.

'That's impossible,' I said.

'There's nothing impossible until you try, sergeant. This mess-up is my responsibility, So!'

'Must I try, sir?'

'Stay with your men,' he said, as he made a dash. I saw him make it round that bend.

I couldn't speak. Everything went quiet. I looked down on the roads below.

'They're coming, our lads are coming. Look—the trucks. Thank Christ,' I uttered with relief. Then the yelling and screaming started—it was the tribesmen. I jumped up and looked round the truck. My heart nearly stopped beating. Through the glare of the sun, I could see them coming down the slope to finish us off. I shouted to the lads,

'Quick, get ready to fire.' It was near impossible with that sun in our eyes. Then a machine-gun opened fire, not at us, but at the tribesmen. It was Captain Holmes, he had got that armoured car in position and was now taking vengeance on these swines who nearly killed us. What a sight to see. They were falling and fleeing in all directions. We all started firing now, regardless of the sun. Every truck with available men did the same. We kept firing, out of relief, and so did that brave and gallant officer of ours, who alone and badly wounded, saved the day.

British troops had arrived, Sikh and Gurkha, and given chase to the tribesmen, pursuing them for miles and taking toll. The tribesmen wouldn't forget this lot in a hurry and, I am afraid, neither would we. Ambulances were taking the dead and wounded away. The lads who had survived this ambush were busy hugging each other in joy, some young soldiers even cried. I know I did when I shook hands with old Ding-Dong Bell, Sergeant Jones and my pal, although a private solidier, Len.

'Where's Jock, Len? Have you seen him?' I asked.

'They've just taken him away, sarge.'

'Was he wounded?'

'No, just dead, bloody dead,' Len said with anger in his voice.

That night, together with Sergeant Bell, 'Ding-Dong' as we affectionately called him, Sergeant Jones and Lieutenant Fox, we drank and talked until the early hours, thanking our lucky stars we had survived, but five had died. It was said later that we were the first troops to survive an ambush like that in the past fifty years on the North-West Frontier of India. We heard, too, that we were leaving this place.

Chapter Eight

THE DAY THE LOCUSTS CAME

One month to the day, we were in camp somewhere in India. It was here that I saw poverty at its worst. It made the depression days back home seem unimportant. India, the land of wealth, of Rajahs' in palaces of gold; a land so fervent in religion, Hindus and Moslems, to each his own; a land so steeped in ceremonies; it made me sick at what I saw and, worse still, at my inability to help.

People were dying in the streets, women with babes in their arms were dying in the gutters, the babes trying to suck their mothers' dry and withered breasts. It was pathetic to see. People walking past seemed so unconcerned at this tragedy in their midst and I felt so ashamed, as a soldier, to have to be one of the people unconcerned. It was impossible for any individual or group to help; it needed the unity of nations.

'It always happens, sahib,' I was told by an affluent Indian, who himself was as fat as a pig. He owned one of the largest restaurants around, which served the finest exquisite foods. It was easy for him to talk, as people died at his door, while his clientele gorged his fine foods.

I saw, myself, the bodies of these starved unfortunates, being ripped apart and eaten by the rabies-ridden dogs that roamed around in packs.

On one occasion, as I left camp one evening with Sergeant Bell, I saw at the gate a little girl around ten years old, sitting with her back to the gatepost. Sergeant Bell and I looked at her as we passed. She held out her hands pleadingly.

'Sahib,' she said, hardly audible, then with her fingers

together, she put them to her mouth.

'God!' I said to Bell, 'Can't we help her?'

'I doubt it,' Bell replied, 'she's too far gone I'm afraid. Come on, let's go.'

I didn't move. I just stared at the girl. She was pretty, her jet-black hair protruded from her tattered sari that draped her body and covered part of her head.

'Wait a minute, Ding-Dong,' I said as I went into the guardroom. 'Have you a bit of rooti, corporal?' I asked ('rooti' meaning bread).

'I think I can scrounge a bit from somewhere,' the corporal replied. 'What's it for, sarge?'

'There's a chico out here and she's bloody starving.'

'Here, will this do?' the corporal asked, handing me a couple of slices of bread. I thanked him and went to the little girl, putting the bread in her lap. She raised her eyes in gratitude and placed her frail little hands on the bread.

'Eat,' I said, 'Rooti good. Come on,' I said to Bell 'let's go. I just can't understand how people are allowed to starve and die like this, especially kids.'

'I've been in India a long time, Spud, and it's been going on for years and years, and will go on, you see.' Bell said, as we walked down the road.

'Well, I don't know, but something's wrong somewhere. I thought we were bad enough in the depression, but this lot here takes the cake,' I said.

'Do you know, Spud, those little kids you see begging, not the ones that run after you for "buckshee", but the horribly twisted-limbed ones that drag themselves along the streets so pathetically—well, their parents have done that damage, so that you will take pity and give.'

'No more, Ding-Dong, I've heard just about enough. Let's have that drink and forget about this lot.'

I never thought of that young girl as we drove through the barrack gate late that night, in a horse-drawn 'ghari'. I'd had a few drinks, and I was tired and probably this was the reason why I had forgotten her.

The next morning was Sunday, a free day. I thought that I would have a run before breakfast, so I washed, put on my P.T. Instructor's gear and set off, intending to do a couple of miles. That would allow me to get back before breakfast.

It was on my return, something caught my eye as I neared the gate. It was only a piece of rag, but it looked familiar. I went over to take a closer look. There was a ditch at the side of the road and strewn round here in this ditch, was what remained of that poor child I had seen at the gate the previous night. That rag I first saw was but a part of her sari, the remainder of it torn to shreds, and the bones of this poor unfortunate creature were stripped bare of her flesh, and lay there in that dusty ditch, crawling with ants.

The wild dogs of India had done the job of the undertaker, without fuss or costs.

I had only been at the camp a week before I heard that I was going on a course for a few days—an amphibious course of five days for officers and N.C.O.s, to learn new techniques in crossing rivers, use of dinghies, etc. I enjoyed it to the full and I certainly learned a lot to pass on to my men. By the end of the course, I was proficient in the use of these crafts.

As we were preparing to return to our unit, I heard that the company office had been warned that locusts were heading in our direction in full flight. I had heard of locusts, a winged creature very similar to the grasshopper, and not dangerous, inasmuch as they weren't carnivorous; yet, wherever they landed, they destroyed every crop and tree in sight.

I didn't pay much attention when I heard about them coming in our direction, and I didn't realize I was about to witness a spectacle that I would remember all my life, and if I lived to be a thousand I might never see it again. I called that day, the day the locusts came.

The first indication I got was the noise, a sort of drone. I ran out of my 'basha' with Bell and Jones. We were only wearing our trunks as it was very hot. Everyone was out. We looked up, shielding our eyes with our hands from that blazing sun. The sky in the distance was black with these winged insects; they stretched as far as the eye could see, and the noise was getting louder.

'Christ, get something in your ears,' Bell said, 'before it deafens us.'

We did so in double quick time. They were getting nearer. I stuffed some cotton wool in my ears but I could still hear them. They seemed to be overhead now, blotting out the sun.

'Thank God, they are going over, Ding-Dong,' I said. He couldn't hear me, he was still gazing upwards. Who could hear with that racket? I couldn't even hear myself speak. Then I noticed that batches of locusts were dropping all around. Just a few. They weren't unlike the grasshoppers we see in England. Could these be scouts signalling to the multitudes in the sky, telling them when and where to come to? I wasn't to wait long to know, for they started to fall, fast and furious. The noise grew louder and louder, and before I knew it they were all around me. It was like a nightmare. I beat at them wildly with my arms. I was covered from head to foot. I couldn't see Bell or anyone else. They blotted out everything. They were in my hair and on my face and completely covered my body. I was frightened—who wouldn't be? It was a terrible sensation to have these creatures, in this amount, all over your body. I was only in my trunks, but as fast as I knocked them off, more alighted on me. How much ground they covered I don't know, but as they thinned out in the air and came down to settle all I saw was one seething mass as far as the eye could see, several inches deep, fighting for the green food, plants, leaves— anything green. I stood ankle deep in them.

I could see Bell and the others, like me, still dazed by this onslaught.

'Grab something to kill them with,' an officer shouted. 'Quick.' We couldn't run because the locusts were so deep. We armed ourselves with brooms and shovels and beat madly at them as fast as we could. Then someone had the brainy idea to spray them with petrol, but as soon as this was organized, and a few set alight, the locusts took to the air in unison, going higher and higher, once again blotting out the sky, but leaving behind their dead and dying.

I stood with Sergeant Bell and an officer watching the locusts as they flew south and beyond sight.

'Now it's the turn for the birds. What a feast they'll have. Look, they're at them now,' the officer said. Sure enough, birds of all kinds were busy eating the locusts.

'Well, that's the finest sight I have ever witnessed,' I said.

'Yes,' said the officer, 'if we live to be a thousand, we might never see a spectacle like that again, never.'

I looked around. There wasn't a bit of greenery left anywhere. It looked as if some force had blasted everything, as the birds kept flying in and picking up their locusts.

'I'm off for a shower. How about it, Spud?' shouted Bell.

'Sure thing,' I said, as I started to walk to the basha.

That evening, the officers came to the Sergeants' Mess for a social evening and the chief topic turned out to be—the day the locusts came.

Chapter Nine

ON LEAVE

We returned to our unit the next day. It took six or seven hours by road and we arrived in our barracks around 4 p.m. Then, as I read company details, I had the surprise of my life, and so did Sergeants Bell and Jones. We had been granted three weeks leave. We just couldn't believe it was true.

'That's bloody great,' Bell said, 'just great. There's a little hill station I know,' he said, rubbing his hands together in delight. 'We can get away from this stinking heat for a while. How about it? Are you game?'

Jones and I just looked at him, then I looked at Jones.

'What's he on about?' I said. 'Hill station?'

'Look, you two bums,' Bell said, 'you forget I'm the old soldier. I've been in India a long time and I know just what I'm talking about. Are you going to trust me and come with me?'

'You're on,' I said, 'and you had better be right, Ding-Dong, or else.'

'Or else what?' he replied, putting his arms round our shoulders. 'Come on, let's see if we can get a drink. We're on leave,' he shouted as we walked to the Mess.

Next morning, we had to get our uniforms ready and pressed, get our passes and rail warrants, and by midday we were on our way.

'We won't get there until tomorrow,' Bell said, 'but I know a good place to stay over night.'

'We'll leave everything to you, Ding-Dong,' I said, 'Right, Jones?'

'Right,' Sergeant Jones replied.

The only thing that took the cream off my excitement was seeing these starving people. The station was full of them begging—it was really pathetic. Sergeant Bell could see I was getting concerned for them, so he promptly said:

'Look here, Spud, don't get involved. I've seen so bloody much of this that I have just got immune to it. There are thousands upon thousands in this plight, year in and year out. What the bloody hell can we do? Just ignore it, for God's sake. You'll have to harden yourself, or you'll not survive your bloody self. Come on, we're on leave,' he said, and grabbed my arm, pulling me to the train.

It was around 9 p.m. that night when the train arrived. It didn't go any farther, and from here we had to travel by road; but that would be tomorrow. Tonight, we were booking into the hotel.

We were up early the next morning and on the bus for the four-hours journey to the hill station, our final destination. We got seats near the driver. As the Indians started to get aboard with their belongings, the bus soon filled up, but they still got on; it didn't matter where or how—soon they were on top and on the sides.

'Christ,' I said, 'what the hell are they doing? They're as bad as the locusts, climbing all over the bus.'

'We're off,' said Sergeant Bell, as the bus gave a lurch forward —the driver had let the clutch out too quickly.

'I only hope he can drive this bloody contraption,' I said.

'You wait, Spud, till we get up the mountain roads. You'll have heart failure when you look down,' Bell said. 'There's many a bus gone down the ravine, full of people.'

'You're just like Al Read,' I said, 'why don't you shut your trap?'

Bell just laughed.

'I can't see out for this lot on the sides,' Jones said, poking a finger at one of the Indians hanging on.

'I'm telling you, you'll not want to look out when we get up farther. Anyhow, you can see enough out of the front.'

We were in low gear as we climbed up and up, twisting and turning up this treacherous narrow road. I thought at times that the bus would roll back at any minute, or fall over the side to land thousands of feet below, for it was precariously close to the edge, too damn close for my liking.

It certainly was beautiful to gaze down to the plains, far, far below, but to tell the truth, I couldn't for the life of me appreciate it, this journey was too perilous. I was relieved when we got to our destination.

'That was bloody awful,' I said as I got off the bus and stretched my legs.

'If you think that was bad, Spud, just wait till we go down,' Bell said. 'I'll lay you fifty rupees you both shit yourself. A bet?'

'Get lost, Ding-Dong, we'll find some other way of getting back.'

Sergeant Bell just laughed and laughed.

'Hey!' I shouted. 'Our kit boxes, before a loose wallah gets 'em. Come on, you two, give us a hand', and I climbed on the bus. 'There they are. Grab hold, you two.'

'We'll grab a taxi,' Bell said. 'Hey, taxi!'

'Taxi, sahib,' as one drew up near us. 'Teeki. Kither Jaga?'

'Union Jack Club, Gilti.'

Off we set, to the club and to start our three weeks leave. I didn't realize then, as I sat in the back seat of that taxi, that this was the beginning of a total love affair with a very beautiful woman, the wife of an officer.

Our first job when we arrived at our quarters, was to have a shower. Believe me, we needed it. We were so dusty from the ride up the mountain road in the bus without windows. The 'boy' unpacked and put our uniforms on coat hangers and polished our shoes, while we were in the showers.

I wore my white 'duck' uniform, while Sergeants Jones and Bell wore their dark dress suits. I felt good as we went down to dinner.

'Just what the doctor ordered,' Bell said as he looked at the menu. 'Three weeks of this and we'll be as fat as pigs.'

After the meal, we sat drinking ice-cold beer and chatting, wondering what we would do tonight.

'Before I do anything, I have to write a letter,' I said. 'You two can wait for me in the bar.'

'I'll bet it's to Kathleen again,' Bell said.

'How did you guess that?' I asked.

They both laughed.

'Who else could it be? You're always writing to her, and I'll bet she's got somebody else by now,' Bell said. 'You don't think she's sitting on her arse doing nothing but waiting for your letters?'

'Speak for yourself,' I said as I got up and went upstairs. 'See you later and don't get drunk.'

One hour later, I was coming downstairs when I heard music, and I thought how good it sounded. I made my way to the bar. I had to go through an archway to get to the bar. There was a dance on, which surprised me. A few couples were on the floor as I went over to the bar.

'I didn't know there was a dance on tonight, did you, lads?' I asked Bell and Jones, as I walked up.

'It surprised us too,' they replied. 'So we might as well stay here, we won't bother to go out,' Ding-Dong said. 'What are you drinking?'

'A pint of the best,' I answered, looking round the dance floor.

'There you are, Spud me boy, how does that look?' Bell said, handing me a pint.

'Just great, just great,' I replied, as I took the cool-looking drink from Bell.

I had just got the drink to my lips, when someone tapped me

on the shoulder. I looked round, the drink nearly falling out of my hand. I liked what I saw very much. A tall, well-made woman with lovely red hair, dressed in a white evening dress that left nothing to the imagination, was standing there.

'I hope you will excuse me,' she said, 'but I noticed that you belong to the same regiment as my husband.'

Bell and Jones moved closer to us.

'What's his name?' Bell asked, trying to get in on the act (I knew Bell only too well).

'Would you like to dance?' I asked, as I took her arm. 'You can tell me as we dance.'

I handed my drink to Jones. She smiled.

'Certainly,' she said, 'I would love to', as she allowed me to take her on to the dance floor.

As I went, I turned round to Bell and Jones and gave a wink. It was a sly wink at that. They both stood there, shaking their fists, a gesture for having fooled them.

'You're safer with me,' I said, as we started to dance.

'Why?' she asked.

'Oh, they would only chase you, you know?'

'And I suppose you won't. Is that it?' she queried.

'Well,' I stammered, 'I must confess, you *are* lovely. What man wouldn't chase you?'

'You cheeky devil,' she replied. 'I might resent you chasing me. My husband's an officer with your lot.'

'What!' I exclaimed, thinking I had put my foot in it. She told me her husband's name.

'Christ,' I said, 'that's torn it. I'm sorry, I didn't know.'

'Oh, don't apologize,' she said, 'and don't let it worry you. I'm sure he will be with someone himself right now, if I know him.'

The music stopped, but I still held on to her as the Sergeant M.C. was announcing another dance.

'I'll tell you what,' she said. 'Why not get a drink and we can sit out on the verandah and talk. It's nice and cool there. What do you say?'

'What do I say?' I repeated. 'I say let's. Come on,' I said, taking hold of her hand and squeezing it. 'But don't go near those two.' I looked over to the bar where I had left Jones and Bell.

'They won't bother us, I don't think,' she said. 'Look, they are talking to a couple of Anglo-Indian girls.'

'So they are. Now we are all happy.'

There were only a few other people on the verandah as we sat down. I didn't speak for a few minutes. I don't know why, but I felt a little guilty, as if I was cheating. I was deep in thought, thinking of Kathleen thousands of miles away, the girl I really and truly loved. What would she think of me now, if she but knew? Sitting here with this beautiful woman, a married woman at that, and me knowing I was going to go to bed with her. I don't know why I knew that, I just sensed it somehow.

'A penny for your thoughts, sergeant,' I heard her say. 'Where have you been to? You were miles away.'

'I'm so sorry. I *was* miles away, thousands of miles at that.'

'Your wife, maybe?' she said.

'No,' I replied, 'it was my girl I was thinking of. She's——'

'I know,' she said, as she put her hand on mine. 'I won't steal you from her, I promise.'

I looked at her.

'What's your first name?' I asked.

'Veronica, but my friends call me Rona. What's yours?'

'Joe, just Joe.'

'Well, Joe,' she said, 'I want you to forget your girl for a little while, just while you are on leave, then we can both enjoy ourselves. Then when your leave is up, we forget we ever knew each other. Agreed?'

I took her hands into mine and pulled her close.

'Agreed,' I said.

She put her face close. I kissed her and she responded with a long lingering kiss, her lips were soft and inviting. I just wanted to love her.

'Did you like that, Joe?' she said, as she sat back and took her drink in her hand. 'Let's drink to a happy time together.'

'That I will,' I replied, picking up my glass.

'This is where you are, you two,' Sergeant Bell said as he walked to our table. 'I thought you had blown.'

By his side stood a girl, holding his hand; an Anglo-Indian girl of remarkable beauty. She, too, was dressed in white, a striking contrast to her dusky features. She was smiling.

'Rona, this is Sergeant Bell. Sergeant Bell, this is Rona.'

Rona and Bell shook hands, then he kissed her on the cheek.

'Enough of that,' I said. 'Now introduce this lovely girl.' I got the shock of my life when Bell said,

'Rona and Joe, this is Maria Decunha. Maria, this is Rona and Joe.'

She smiled and her eyes seemed to light up and speak.

'Pleased to meet you Maria, do you live here?'

Maria just nodded.

'Don't you speak, then?' I said, laughing. She shook her head.

'I—er——' I was lost for words.

'She can't speak,' Sergeant Bell said, 'She's deaf and dumb.'

Well, I could have cut my tongue out for saying what I'd said. I hurriedly apologized.

'Don't worry,' Bell said. 'She understands every word you say. That's right, Maria, isn't it?'

Maria again nodded and smiled. She certainly understood.

'Drink, sahib?' the bearer said as he came to our table.

'Yes, please. Two gin-and-limes and two pints.'

'Teeki, sahib,' the bearer said.

'Come on,' I said to Bell and Maria. 'Sit down, let's all get to know one another. Where's Jones?'

'He went off with Maria's friend.'

'Trust Jones,' I quipped.

It was midnight when I was in the horse-drawn ghari with Rona, heading home, a distance of two miles. It was a lovely fresh evening, the sort you can only get high up in the hills. Rona didn't have any trouble getting past the sentry to her quarters, that were strictly out of bounds to soldiers; strictly, that is, if you didn't have influence like Rona must have had.

'Goodnight, sentry,' she called.

'Goodnight ma'am,' he replied.

The ghari stopped outside her bungalow.

'This is it,' Rona said. I filled with apprehension when she continued, 'Are you coming in then? I won't eat you.'

'It'll be all right?' I asked as I got out of the ghari.

'Of course it will be all right,' she replied. 'You won't get into any trouble, if that's what you mean.'

The lights were on as we went indoors. Rona called out in Urdu which, apparently, she spoke fluently,

'Fatima, aap ja sakti hain—mey ghar khu.' (Meaning You can go now—I'm home.)

'Salaam, mem-sahib,' Fatima replied as she passed me, covering her face.

'Salaam,' Rona replied. 'Now we are alone. I will just get these things off', pointing to her dress, as she went into another room which was divided by a net curtain. I stood there as she undressed, the net curtain giving the situation a touch of eastern magic.

'Get yourself a drink,' she called out, 'and make yourself comfortable. The drinks are in the cabinet.'

I was shaking as I took off my uniform jacket and tie and put them on a chair. I walked over to the cabinet.

'Get me one, please Joe. Gin and lime. You will get some ice in the icebox in the kitchen.'

After I had got the drinks and ice, I sat down on the settee, placing Rona's drink on the coffee table. I took one gulp of my drink.

'That's better,' I thought, 'I needed that. I must get another one.'

The cabinet was full of drinks of all types. As I filled my glass again, I could hear the shower. 'That's what I could do with,' I thought. With the glass in my hand, I walked round the room, just noseying. The shower stopped.

'The shower is free now,' Rona called out. 'Would you like one?' She must have read my thoughts. I didn't have to be asked twice. I undressed and got in that shower quickly. It was great.

'There's a dressing-gown and a bath-towel here for you when you've finished,' Rona said. 'The dressing-gown might be a bit big, but I'm sure it will do.'

'Thanks, I won't be long.'

'O.K. I'll get some coffee on and see what sandwiches Fatima has done.'

I felt on top of the world as I dried myself and splashed eau-de-cologne on my body. The dressing gown was oriental, brightly coloured and in a light material. I looked in the mirror on the wall and combed and groomed my hair.

'You lucky so-and-so,' I said to myself. 'What did you do to deserve this. It's bloody marvellous.'

Rona was just putting the sandwiches and coffee on the small table near the settee as I walked in.

'You do look handsome,' she said, 'even though the dressing-gown is big.'

'And you look ravishing,' I said. I put my arms round her and held her close. Her warm body burned through my dressing-gown.

'You're lovely,' I said, 'really you are.'

She pushed me away, gently.

'Sit down. Have a little supper first. We have all night for that,' she said, smiling.

After two small sandwiches and a coffee, that was enough, her presence near me prevented me from eating more.

Can I get another whisky?' I asked.

'Of course you can. Never ask, just help yourself. Get me one too, please, and let's have some music,' Rona said, as she got off the settee and went across the room.

We sat for ages on the settee, holding hands and just talking and it was quite late when we went to bed.

Rona was a great lover. I lacked the experience, but I was soon to learn everything that night from a lovely woman who did not think it was wrong to love a man other than her husband. I probably thought I was doing wrong, in fact, I knew it was wrong, for I was deeply in love with my Kathleen— and Rona, she was married to someone I knew, but what could I do? I was as weak as a kitten in her presence, and when she loved, she loved totally.

After that first night, my longing for her grew, even though I knew that it wouldn't last, and that if it hadn't been me, it would have been someone else. It was a leave I will never forget. I lived with Rona for three glorious weeks. We played tennis, we went horse-riding and swimming, we went dancing. No matter what we did or where we went, it was Rona at the end of the day to love me and make me forget.

I met Sergeant Bell about twice during my leave. He was with Maria, the beautiful Anglo-Indian girl who was deaf and dumb, and if any couple ever loved each other truly, then it was Bell and Maria. He told me himself, that he intended to marry her.

'Spud,' he said, as we were having a drink one evening, 'I will marry Maria as soon as the war is over. I swear it. You see, she is definitely the one for me.'

'Well, I hope you do, Ding-Dong, I hope you do. She's certainly very pretty.'

We hadn't been in the club an hour when we had a freak hailstorm. We heard a terrible clatter on the road then a roar of thunder so loud, it nearly burst our eardrums. Rona covered her ears; and poor Maria, she just smiled, but the smile soon left her face when a most vivid flash of lightning seemed to cut across the room. Then she realized something was wrong. She and Rona both looked frightened. It only lasted a few minutes, then it was all over, as quick as it had started. Someone from the doorway shouted,

'Just look at this bloody lot. What a mess.'

Bell and I ran outside to see just what was a mess.

'Christ Almighty, look at this,' Bell said, as he picked up a lump of ice, easily as big as a half-brick.

'Hell,' I said. 'That hasn't fallen from the sky, surely. It's impossible.

'Well, it bloody has done. Just look out there.'

Ice blocks were all over the place. A ghari was smashed, and a horse in its shafts lay on the road, quite still. Roofs of some buildings were also damaged and it was not until later that we heard that ten people had also been killed.

As we went to Maria's home for supper, Bell said:

'That's one for the book. I've never seen anything like that before and never will again.'

The time came for our departure from this hill station—our 'Shangri-la'. Jones, the sly fox, wouldn't say how he had spent his leave, but we could guess.

'This is the part I dread, Ding-Dong,' I said, 'this bloody drive down this precarious road.'

'Just close your eyes,' Bell said, 'and you won't see or know anything until we're down on the plains.'

Believe me, that's just what I did, as we sped down the winding road in a cloud of dust. I didn't really close them out of fear of that awful journey, but to think of the wonderful time I had spent with Rona. It was like coming back from heaven, to stark reality.

'Thanks, Rona, for a wonderful time,' I said in my thoughts. 'But now it seems you never existed at all. You are behind me, now and for ever. I can never say I loved you. I just wanted you as you wanted me. Now I wonder who else you will make happy for a little while.'

I contented myself with my thoughts, for they were going back a long way, back to Kathleen and that old oak tree. Goodbye, Rona, and thanks.

There was a lot of activity back at the barracks when we arrived, and we soon learned why.

Our battalion was getting ready to move, this time into the unknown jungles of Burma—at long last.

Our first stepping-stone before we really knew, was Chittagong, a small place in Bengal.

Chapter Ten

BURMA

Chittagong—the assembly place and gateway to Burma, known to soldiers moving up to the front as 'the point of no return'.

There wasn't very much time for relaxing here, getting everything ready, and I mean everything—mules, transport, guns, etc.—it was a hive of activity.

From Chittagong, it meant we had to go so far up a river into Assam. From there, it would be slogging; from lessons learned the hard way in previous defeats by the Japs, it was decided by our Commanders that penetration in the mountainous jungle terrain should be on foot, the most efficient and quickest way, with just small trucks conveying essential stores, also heavily-laden pack mules, the latter being essential.

Flat water craft carried us up the river, each one loaded to capacity. After a few hours, we disembarked somewhere in Assam, a place near Cox's Bazaar, where we set up our camp.

We were part of the 7th Indian Division who were soon to experience some very heavy fighting. In fact, we were the first troops in Burma to defeat the Japs at their own game, when we turned near-defeat into victory, as the Japs were hell-bent on destroying us. That, I believe, was their orders and, by God, they nearly did it.

It was early evening when we made camp, quite near the river and as it was at this part a safe enough place, a few of us went in for a swim in the nude. It was great fun while it lasted but, I'm afraid, short-lived.

We had been in the water about ten minutes, when someone shouted,

'Get out quick.'

They *meant* quick as well, for a few lads started to shout without knowing why, but thinking it was the Japs coming, we all made a dash for the east bank.

'For Christ's sake, hurry your bloody selves. Look—bloody crocodiles will have you.'

I didn't look until I was out of that water and on terra firma —no, sir!—not when I heard them shout 'crocs'. Then I saw them, gliding menacingly towards us.

'I think everyone is out,' an officer said, looking up and down the river. 'Now get clear from the edge. Those damn things can come on land and grab you, Sergeant,' he said to me, 'just make sure everyone is careful not to go too near.'

'Right, sir,' I said. 'I don't think they will need a second telling, not after that scare.'

I got dressed and put my groundsheet up for the night. I intended to get some sleep, as we would be moving most probably at first light the next morning. We were bivouacking, so I fixed my groundsheet like a small tent. Later that night, I thought I'd get my head down. As I started to settle myself in this contraption, I let out a yell. I jumped up, taking the whole lot with me. I had felt something bite me and I really thought it was a snake, the same kind that had killed the Indian bearer on the North-West Frontier—the crate.

I was scared stiff. I just ran to the M.I. tent.

'I've been bit. Quick someone, help me.' Sergeant Jackson ran out of the tent.

'What's wrong, Spud?' he asked.

'I think a crate has bitten me. Do something, for God's sake,' I said, as I started to undo my trousers. Sergeant Jackson pulled them down.

'Bend over,' he said. 'Let's see your arse.' He started to pinch my bottom, looking for the puncture holes. 'Keep still, you silly bugger, while I look!'

I was going frantic and sweating profusely.

'Here it is, Spud. Calm down, it's not a snakebite, thank God. It looks like a scorpion sting.'

'Thank God, you say, Jacko. Thank God, *I* say, I can tell you.'

'Go and lay on that stretcher, Spud, face down. I'll get that sting out.'

Sergeant Jackson, better known as Taffy, was a very good M.I. Sergeant and I could trust him with my life. In fact, he had proved himself on the Frontier, when they brought casualties in after that ambush. He was as good as any doctor.

'You're going to be in pain for a few hours, you know that? I'll give you an injection to help you along,' Taffy said as he pulled the sting out. 'There it is, a scorpion alright.'

'Better than a bleeding snakebite. I'd have been a gonner by now,' I replied.

Taffy laughed.

'More likely the snake would die, biting you.'

'Get the bloody injection done,' I said, 'and save the jokes. I'm feeling some pain now. You're sure there's no danger?'

'To be truthful, Spud, there is a risk; but you're fit, fitter than most of us,' Taffy said. 'It's if you are run down, then it's dangerous. Anyhow, you'd better stay here tonight, and I can see to you.'

'It's not because you fancy me, is it, Taff, you randy sod?' I said with a grin that I forced. 'Ouch!' I shouted as Taff slapped my arse and stuck the needle in.

'That'll change your tune,' he said as he withdrew the needle and dabbed the spot with cotton wool. 'I'll find you a blanket because, by Christ, you're going to sweat, so keep it over you.'

'Don't worry, Taff, I will. Christ, it's painful,' I said, clenching my fist and gritting my teeth.

I don't know for how long I was in pain, but it seemed ages. It was like a nightmare, the sound of the crickets seemed to be so loud and I was so hot. I must have been delirious, sweat was pouring from me, but I remember Taff giving me a drink.

The next thing I remembered was being woken by Taffy. The Medical Officer was with him. I looked around the tent, and then at the M.O.

'How are you this morning, sergeant?' the M.O. asked.

'Fine, sir,' I replied. 'Really fine', I sat up.

'No more pain?' the M.O. asked.

'No, sir, none.'

'Then you will be O.K.,' the M.O. said. 'You've nothing to worry about. You can get up now, but take it steady for a couple of hours.' As he walked away, he said, 'Don't forget next time, watch where you sit down.'

'I will that, sir, and thanks,' I said. I was so relieved that I was O.K.

'Thanks, Taff, thanks a lot,' I said to Sergeant Jackson as he came back into the tent. 'And do you know something, Taff? It's my bloody birthday. I'm twenty-three.'

It was dawn the following morning when my battalion moved on, right into that stinking jungle, where we were soon to learn that only the fittest would survive. We weren't just fighting the Japs, but the elements too, and all the diseases that go with it— malaria, cholera, dysentery, smallpox, typhus, and heat exhaustion.

We marched and rested, marched and rested, through jungle, through swamp. We were moving to position deep in the Arakan. Day after day we moved, just resting for a couple of hours. Our feet were sore and blistered and bleeding; these, we had to see to on the rest period—sore or not, we still marched, or I should say, slogged our way in places.

After days of this, we eventually got to our place of encampment, a base we would operate from and send out patrols. That march had surely been a test of endurance and quite a few men had collapsed, from heat exhaustion and cerebral malaria. But no matter where I was, from leaving England to being in the jungle, I had never forgotten to write to Kathleen, and up till now I had received letters from her. Getting letters was so very important to the men. When the mail orderly brought it round, it was one mad rush. We stood there, officers, N.C.O.s and men, just waiting for the orderly to call out our names and what a relief to hear your own name called. This ritual made men happy; that is, when they received a letter, but it also brought unhappiness for those whose names were not called out.

But worst of all was when a soldier got a letter and he would be waving it about in the air and going to a quiet spot to read it, quite excited, only to get bad news when he read it. One soldier I knew well had received such a letter. His wife, two children and his mother had been killed in an air raid. To see him was pathetic. He went out of his mind. From that happy soldier of only a few minutes earlier, he had been reduced to a babbling object of humanity.

And how many soldiers had read their letters to find that their wives had left them for someone else! Yes, letters, our only link with home, were always happy things to get—or, at least, we hoped they would be.

My first sighting of the Japs came in the form of a patrol, a 'Recce' patrol. It was quite nerve-racking to set off, to go into the unknown, not knowing just how far or how near they were to us, but I was in charge of this patrol, and I was full of enthusiasm as we set off; our objective, some foothills in the Valley, to dig in and observe. I had no idea just how good the Japs were at their jungle warfare, but as time went on I soon realized we were just amateurs.

I wasn't very happy at having one soldier with me called Billings. He was a loudmouth and a bully, and I knew he didn't like me; in fact, he didn't like authority at all. This man weighed about 11 stone to my mere 9 stone 8 lb, and I knew

116

that he thought he could thrash me. He did say this, on one occasion when I charged him with an offence and he got confined to barracks. But I knew that I was fit and quick and he was fat and slow, so I never was scared to give him an order and he knew it, and it annoyed him so.

My patrol was only small—myself, and seven men, consisting of a corporal, lance-corporal signalman and five O.R.s; Len, my old buddy, was one of them and he was a good lad to have around. On our second day out, a violent storm broke out. In five minutes or less, we were just like drowned rats, taking whatever cover we could. We put our capes on, even though we were soaked to the skin. The whole area became a quagmire in minutes.

'You should have kept to the bloody roads,' Billings shouted as we sat in the bush waiting for the rain to stop. Lightning was flashing every few seconds. I knew it was useless to go on in this lot and the best thing to do was to stay there. I ignored his remark.

'Sergeants? I've shit 'em,' Billings said again. 'I bet you don't know where we are do you?'

'In fact, I don't, Billings; but I know this much, you have to depend on me.'

'Don't let him worry you, sarge. Christ, things are bad enough,' Len said. 'You should've left him back at camp. He does nothing only shout his mouth off.'

'Listen to creepy fuckin' Crawley,' Billings sneered.

'You've said enough, Billings. Just button your lip or I'll——'

'You'll what, sergeant? Put me on a charge? Will I get C.B. here in this stinking rotten hole?' Billings retorted angrily 'Good. It'll be better than meeting these little yellow bastards. Go on, sarge boy, charge me.'

'That's it,' I said. I was livid. I had just had enough of Billings and now I didn't care about Japs or my rank. I knew that Billings had to be taught a lesson or my authority would just go.

'Put that under your cape, Len,' I said, handing him my Sten gun. The rain was pelting down from the heavens and I was ankle deep, in mud, and as I went forward, I slipped. I was covered in mud from head to foot, but I threw myself at Billings like a wild cat. I hit him full on his nose as he tried to get up, then he grabbed my cape at the collar and pulled me down. I was still thumping at him as the lads got hold of me and pulled me up, two of them holding on to Billings. He just looked at me, flabbergasted.

'What the bloody hell are you thinking of sarge?' Len asked. 'Doing a thing like that—you could lose your stripes for this little lot.'

'I couldn't give a damn. That bloke is a bloody menace,' I replied. 'He can report it when we get back, if we ever do. If he shouts like he has been doing, we'll all be done in, that's for sure.'

Billings was still staring at me.

'Get off you two,' he said to the two still holding him down.

'You won't start anything?' they said.

'Course not.'

The two lads released their hold on him. Then he did a surprising thing. As he sat up, he held out his hand to me and said, 'Sorry, sarge. Can we forget a report?'

'What report?' I said, smiling and taking his muddy hand in mine.

'Yes,' he replied, 'what report?' and laughed.

'Do you know something, sarge? It's stopped bloody raining while we've been pissing about.'

'You're right. Get your capes off and let's get moving.'

That little episode was never mentioned again by any one of us, and Billings, although I never doubted his capabilities as a soldier, proved to be one of the best. A few months after, in a big battle with the Japs, he died fighting and shouting, when they broke through our defences. I saw him standing there, bawling out, 'Come on you little yellow-bellies. Fight!', when he was run through with a Japanese bayonet.

We reached our position in fading light that day, some high ground with plenty of cover, overlooking the valleys below. Our first task was to dig our slit trenches and cover them with bracken when we were in them. That way, we could sleep until first light. But sleep I never got. Huddled up in that narrow little slit trench, we only got snatches of sleep, as we took turn to keep watch. Many's the time we were scared stiff, not daring to make a sound, as something could be heard prowling around. It was probably some animal that could smell us.

The night seemed so long, and I really thought that daylight would never come. Every hour seemed like a day. I must have dozed off, for the lance-corporal signalman who was in my trench, woke me.

'Sarge,' he whispered, 'sarge, there's someone out there.' I wakened with a start.

'What! What!' I said, rubbing my eyes. 'Where?'

'Amongst those bushes, right in front of us,' the corporal said. I peered through the leaves of our camouflage, straining my eyes and frightened to close them. Then I saw a face, I know I did, and it looked like a Jap. My heart beat twenty to the dozen, yet I knew that I had to make a decision. I was responsible for this patrol, and I meant to do something, otherwise it would be too damn late. Hadn't I learned that lesson on the Frontier from my Captain?

'Take this Sten gun,' I whispered to the corporal, 'and be ready to fire if they rush you. I'll go out there and see, after I warn the others. For Christ's sake, don't fire until they do rush you, because I'm out there,' I said. 'Have you got that?'

'Right, sarge,' the corporal said, a little nervously.

I quickly got out of the trench at the back of our camouflage, and crawled round to each slit trench to warn the lads to be ready to fire.

'I bleedin' hope they don't think I'm a Jap and start to fire at me,' I thought as I slowly worked my way round each one, and told them just what to expect. I then crawled forward and into the bushes where I had seen that face. I waited with baited breath as I drew my knife. There was someone behind that bush all right. I heard it rustle, and it wasn't the wind because there wasn't any. I tensed myself, ready to plunge my knife, when a goat came out, followed by a small Burmese boy with a stick in his hand.

'Thank God,' I said to myself as the little boy hit the goat with the stick and shouted something in Burmese. I waited until he had gone, then crawled back to the slit trenches to tell the lads.

'Better safe than sorry,' I said to them.

'I thought there was a bloody patrol of Japs out there, sarge, the way you come and told us to be ready to fire,' the corporal said. 'Anyhow, I suppose there could have been and I'm glad it was only a bleeding goat. What time is it, sarge?' he said. I looked at my watch.

'O-six-hundred hours,' I replied. 'Will you get someone to rustle up some tea.'

'I'll get it sarge,' Billings said. 'Just leave it to me.'

That day was spent quietly and inconspicuously, observing the whole area with binoculars.

It was later that evening that I got my first glimpse of the Japs. I was sure they were Japs—our troops weren't up this far.

There was some activity going on about two miles away at the far end of the valley. With my binoculars to my eyes, I began to focus on one spot where I had first seen movement. I could see soldiers and mules, fully laden with equipment. They only came into view at a certain spot, then disappeared. I counted as best I could. There were at least fifty soldiers and the same number of mules. A supply route. I quickly worked out the reference point on my map, telling the corporal to keep them under observation.

I ordered my signalman to get word back by mirror signal, of this Jap movement in this area. This signal was acknowledged and we were ordered back to base.

I vacated our position at dusk and started back, our task here completed.

I was a good mile away when I decided to bivouac for the night. My men were tired and so was I and it would be better to start back at first light when we could move faster. We found what good spot we could that offered concealment and comfort. This was the jungle, that held untold dangers that we didn't expect—this we had to put up with and we got used to. Except for the heat and the mosquitoes that we were for ever swotting, we managed quite well to reach base without mishap. Living on K rations wasn't very good and at least we got a cooked meal of stew that went down well, even if we didn't know what was in it—and anyway, we didn't care!

I never knew whether our information was accepted or ignored as unlikely, for it was but a few days later when we were caught napping, in the form of Jap soldiers dressed as Gurkhas. Somehow, they had infiltrated our lines and caused havoc. It was a hit-and-run affair. Once they were in our lines, they had been allowed to pass unmolested, our men thinking they were Gurkha troops. What a bloody blunder! And bloody it was—they caused a lot of damage and casualties before being driven off.

That was a night to remember and another lesson learned the hard way.

From then on, it was patrol after patrol, and every report coming in was acted upon—there was no relaxing. It was a matter of 'do unto them as they do unto you'. My mate, Sergeant Bell, got promotion. He was now my Sergeant-Major and I was glad. He deserved it, for he was a good soldier and a good leader. Sergeant Jones won the Distinguished Conduct Medal after a patrol duty. He had encountered the Japs, and with only a few men, had inflicted many casualties on them with the loss of four of his men. He then got the remainder back safely.

So it was a night of celebration for Bell, Jones and me as we quietly sat drinking rum that Bell had somehow got hold of.

'I'm going to get pissed tonight for sure,' Bell said as he poured some rum into my mess can and some into Jones's. 'I couldn't care bloody less. Fancy getting promotion here, in this godforsaken rat hole. It's only a matter of time before we all fucking perish, I know, the way things are going.'

'What do you mean, Ding-Dong—we'll all perish?' I said.

'What I say,' Bell replied. 'Just look at the spaces in our ranks, where soldiers once stood.'

'Come-on, Ding-Dong,' Jones said, 'change the subject. Tell me, do you ever hear from Maria?'

'Hear from her? Hear from her did you say?' Bell said in a slurred voice. 'Course I bloody hear from her. I was going to marry that girl, let me tell you. She was the best thing that ever happened to me.'

He grabbed hold of the bottle of rum to pour out another drink.

'No more for me, Ding-Dong, and you've had enough too,' Jones said.

'How about you, Spud? One for the road?'

'No thanks, Ding-Dong, let's call it a night,' I replied. 'I'm on patrol tomorrow with old Foxy, so I'll need some shut-eye.'

'I'll finish this bottle and then sleep it off. I'll dream of Maria instead of those bastard slant-eyes.'

'Goodnight, you two, I'm off,' I said, 'and don't forget to see that Ding-Dong gets under cover,' I said to Jones.

'Goodnight, Spud, and good luck tomorrow.'

I nodded. 'See you in a few days.'

With that, I went off to my little tent. It was a clear night and just the sound of crickets disturbed the peace, and the flapping wings of the vampire bats, as they flew aimlessly round.

I thought that at any minute, one would fly into me, they came so low. I hated the sight of these creatures. We called them flying foxes—they were so big. I saw one once, that some of the lads had caught, and it certainly looked like a fox, with a wing-span of over two feet. I looked up and said, 'This is your rotten home, not mine.' Then I crawled into my little haven of rest.

It was around 0700 hours when our patrol left. I wasn't one bit worried. I had a good officer and corporal, Nobby Clark, a true cockney and a good bloke to have around; and there was Len (I liked Len a lot—I suppose it was because we had trained together as recruits) and eight other good lads, making twelve in all.

We had been out about three days without seeing a thing, then we started to cross some paddy fields.

'Are we wise, sir, going across here?' I asked. 'We're in the open too much for my liking.'

'I don't like it myself,' Foxy said, 'but it's the only way. My objective is those hills over there at forty-five degrees. A thousand yards or so and we will be under cover again. Deploy your men,' Foxy said. 'You're not scared, are you, Spud?' he smiled as he said it. The smile was still on his face as he was hit. He uttered two words, 'Christ Almighty', as his stomach was ripped open and his guts fell out. He fell into the water and rice crops of the paddy fields. I fell at his side, shouting to the men to take cover. The Japs couldn't see us now as we lay in the water and crops, but they were still firing. I lifted Foxy's face out of the water and pulled him round. What a bloody mess he was with his intestines hanging out.

'You bloody fool, Foxy,' I said as I kept low and held his head in my arm. I said it with emotion and not anger or contempt at his mistake.

'Get out of it, Spud, get out,' Foxy murmured.

'Not without you, we won't leave you, I promise.'

123

Foxy smiled again. 'Thanks, Spud,' he said, 'I'll rec— —',
then his voice faded.

The Japs started to fire again. It was a machine gun, but
they had lost our position—the bullets were falling short now.

'Nobby, are you there?' I asked in a loud sort of whisper.

'Coming, sarge,' Nobby replied.

'Give us a lift. Mr. Fox has been hit,' I said. Nobby crawled
through the rice crops to my side.

'Brett's dead, sarge,' he said.

'Are you sure?'

'I'm sure. I don't know if there's anyone else though.'

'Get the other side and hook your arm under Foxy's. I'll
do the same, then we can crawl back with him.'

As we started to move, I called out to the lads.

'Crawl back to cover. Do you hear me? Get back. Right,
Nobby, keep going, it isn't far.'

We both strained and pulled, then there was another burst
of fire. I felt a thud on my leg.

'I've been hit, Nobby,' I said, 'in the leg.'

'Can you manage?' Nobby asked.

'Yes, keep going for God's sake or we've all had it.'

It seemed an eternity as we pulled and crawled our way to
cover, but we made it, right into the undergrowth where we
lay breathless for a while.

'Nobby, just check on the lads, quick,' I said, 'but for Christ's
sake, keep down yourself. Get them over here.'

Nobby nodded and, like a snake, he crawled away. I looked
at my leg. A bullet had gone through my calf and out at the
front just missing my shin bone. I looked at Leiutenant Fox.

'He's dead,' I said to myself; 'he's bloody dead. We've been
dragging a dead man.'

My leg was paining me now.

'Come on Nobby, where the hell are yer?' I said as I looked
around me. 'God, don't those crickets ever stop making that
noise?' I thought. I started to think on what Sergeant-Major

Bell had said the other night, that we were all going to perish. What of the wild animals that roamed around at night? Would they attack me and the dead body of Foxy? Were those bloody Japs coming, knowing that we were here? I brought my Sten gun to a firing position, then I heard Nobby calling. Thank God!

'O.K., sarge,' he called, 'It's Nobby. Brett's dead and Ginger is missing, otherwise all present.'

'Right, we'll have to get moving,' I said.

'Yes, when I've seen to your leg,' Nobby replied, and he got a field dressing out of his pocket and began to rip my trouser leg.

'It's not too bad, sarge, it looks clean,' he said, as he dressed it. 'How does it feel?'

'Just throbbing bad, but it's gangrene or tetanus I'll worry about now,' I said.

'I'll take another look at it when we get out of this bleeding hole and get further back.'

'Foxy's dead,' I said.

'I knew that before I looked for the lads,' Nobby said. 'Poor sod.'

'Detail two of the lads to bury him quick. I don't like leaving him like this. Get his identity disc and anything he has and then take somebody with you and have a scout round for Ginger. He could be lying out there wounded. Make it quick, and, Nobby—be careful,' I said.

We buried Lieutenant Fox as best we could, just leaving a marker on his grave.

'No sign of Ginger, sarge,' Nobby said as he came back.

'O.K., let's move quickly,' I said, and I made the sign of the cross over Foxy's grave. 'You know the score, get us back.'

Nobby immediately shouted,

'Come on, you lot, let's get your arses out of here. Len, you go ahead about ten or fifteen yards. You know what to do.'

'O.K., corporal,' Len replied.

It was a bedraggled nine men that set off back, weary, hungry men and me with one good leg. As we left, I looked back at Foxy's grave and my eyes filled with tears.

We must have gone five miles or more before we rested; first and foremost, to get the leeches off our backs—those horrible slimy creatures that thought we were blood donors. The only way I ever knew to get them off was by touching them with a lighted cigarette. I often wondered whether it was the burn they didn't like or the smell of those horrible Victory V cigarettes. How we ever stuck them, I'll never know.

'It'll be dark soon, Nobby,' I said. 'This spot is as good as any to kip down. What do you think?'

'I'll just have a look around first,' Nobby replied, 'after we've checked our position.'

'O.K., fine.'

'How s your leg?' Nobby asked.

'It bloody well hurts,' I replied, as I squeezed my calf.

'I'll take a look at it as soon as I can,' Nobby said.

'Here, I'll do that,' Len said.

'O.K., Nobby,' I called out, 'just see to the lads, will yer? Make sure everybody's alright and let me know if we're O.K. for water'

'I'm sure we are, but I'll check,' Nobby said, then went off.

'What do you think of this lot, Len?' I said as he put a clean bandage on my leg. 'Those bloody mosquitoes don't let up, do they?' I said, swotting them on my face and neck. 'You haven't answered me Len.'

Len just looked at me. I said it again.

'What do you think of this lot, being here in this bloody jungle?'

'If you really want to know how I feel, sarge, well, I feel we'll never get out of this. It seems to go on and on: this patrol, that patrol; pull back here and pull back there. If we could get on the offensive and not the defensive, I'd feel better. How does that feel?' he said, as he tied my bandage.

'Great, Len, just great, and call me Spud; it'll do here. And don't worry about getting out of this jungle or beating the Japs;

we'll do it, Len, I'm sure. We've just got to do, and don't forget, you've a wife and kid to go home to some day.'

'That's just what worries me, Spud, I'm telling you.'

'Do you know, I haven't had a letter for months from my girl, so she might have met somebody else. I've decided not to write any more. She hasn't answered mine for ages.'

'Everything's O.K., sarge. We're alright here. The lads are settled and I've put two men on watch,' Nobby said coming towards me. 'You can get a bit of shut-eye, Len, and you, sarge. I'll do two to three hours' watch, then give you a shake. We can get started then at first light and, on my reckoning, we could be at base late afternoon.'

'Great, Nobby,' I said. 'Don't forget to give me a nudge', then I settled myself in a sitting position with my back to a tree. I closed my eyes and slept.

We moved out as soon as it was light enough to see. The trek back was slow and uneventful, and we reached our base at around 1800 hours. We were so thankful to get there. From the time we knew we were near, all I could hear from the lads was, 'It'll be great to get a mug of char and some cooked grub.' We all knew that the grub wasn't that bloody good, but after a week on K rations, Davenport's stew (he was the company cook) would be great even though we never found out what he put in it.

My report made out, my leg attended to, I had a good wash and change of clothes from those louse-ridden ones and I felt a new man. I thanked God my leg wound was clean and would heal nicely.

The news of the loss of Lieutenant Fox, Brett and Ginger was received with silence. Two days later I got a great surprise. Ginger, the lad who was missing on our patrol, had arrived back on his own. What had happened to him that day we were fired on, or how he managed to get back, I'll never know. It was a marvellous feat for someone without compass or bearing to do this. He was certainly the worse for wear and shocked, and I believe he was sent to the hospital further back for treatment.

Days went by and I saw a few patrols go out and come back. I couldn't go because of my leg wound, but it was on the mend.

One evening, I was sitting on my own, scribbling a letter to my mam and dad, when I thought on Len's words, about not getting out of the jungle and just doing patrols and no offensive. This decided me to write a little poem that I still have today. I called it

Men of the Arakan

These men of the Arakan,
They did their job to a man.
They lived, they fought, at times they ran,
These men of the Arakan.

We youths of the Empire
Were sent out to trap
This mighty horde they call the Jap.
We will do it, do it well.
What Regiments, I cannot tell.
Just call us men of the Arakan,
We will do our job, every man,
We will fight or die, like a soldier can,
Right here, for you, in the Arakan.

Before long, there was a drive
Made by the allies, let loose like bees from a hive.
Through jungle and swamps, cities and ghats,
They stopped for ever, the plague of the Japs.

Chapter Eleven

THROUGH HELL AND BACK

That night, after I settled down to sleep, I got a very uneasy feeling that I can't describe. I lay awake for a long time. The sound of the crickets and the laugh of the *hyena*, that ugly and ferocious animal that usually leads a pack of hungry *jackals* on a rampage of death, only added to my uneasiness.

Although I was fully clothed, I felt cold. I pulled my blankets round me and closed my eyes, and directed my thoughts back home to my family and Kathleen. I wanted to shut out the nightmare, for that is what it was—a horrible nightmare that went on and on and was getting worse. Just now, I felt at my lowest ebb.

What I would give to be a kid again, back home with my brothers, to be in that brass-knobbed iron bed, snuggled in between them where I always felt safe. And Frank would ask me to scratch his back.

'I'll give yer a penny on Friday,' he would say, 'if yer'll scratch it.'

That promise from Frank did the trick. When I'd finished, I would turn to Jim.

'Will yer tell me a story, Jim?' I would say.

'I'm tired, go to sleep,' he answered.

'Please, Jim, just one.'

'I suppose you won't let me go to sleep until I do, will yer? What do you want?'

'Johnny and his little bull,' I'd say. I always liked that story, although Jim had told it to me hundreds of times. Where were my brothers now? In the Middle East perhaps? In a prison camp somewhere, or maybe, like me, here in Burma? Worse still, they could have been killed! I started to sweat now.

'No!' I shouted. 'No, not dead.' Tears squeezed through my closed eyes as I controlled my thoughts and started to pray.

'Please God, keep my brothers safe, bring the war to an end, before we all perish. Please God.' I felt for my crucifix that hung round my kneck and kissed it. I then thought of Kathleen and wondered why I hadn't received any letters from her. There she was, smiling at me.

'Kathleen,' I said, and then she disappeared. Had anything happened to her? Something must be wrong, because I was so sure she loved me. Why hadn't she written?

I must have fallen asleep, as I saw her so plainly, standing at the window, waving to me as the train took me away from her. I shouted out loud as I stretched my hands out to hold her. I sat up with a start. It was light now. A voice said,

'It's o-five-thirty hours, sarge. Wakey wakey.'

'Right,' I said, as I ran my fingers through my hair and realized where I was. Had I lain down last night and thought about home, or was it a dream? I never knew.

I jumped out and poured a little water from a 'chugal' (a canvas bag used for carrying water) into my mess tin, to wash. There was only enough to get the sleep out of your eyes as water was very precious and it had to be used sparingly— a thing you treated with the greatest respect here in Burma.

I was cleaning my Sten gun when C.S.M. Bell came towards me.

'Company H.Q. right after grub,' he said to me.

'Right, I'll be there,' I replied.

'Right what?' he barked back. I looked at him with surprise for a moment as he stood there. He looked different, I don't know how, but he just looked different. I was just about to ask him what was wrong, when he again shouted, more menacingly, 'Right what?'

The words stumbled out from my lips, 'Right, sir.'

He muttered something as he walked away.

'Christ,' I said to myself, 'what's wrong with Ding-Dong? Is he mad?'

How true these words were to become later on.

It was at the field kitchen as I stood with Sergeant Jones, waiting to get our breakfast of a soya sausage and some dehydrated potato, that I said, 'What's wrong with Ding-Dong?'

'That's just what I was thinking too,' Jones replied. 'It could be battle fatigue, I suppose, or most likely, malaria coming on again.'

'It's something,' I said, 'or he's going round the bleeding bend. He should see the quack before we move out. It'll be bad enough where we're going without putting up with his tantrums. Is that all we get?' I said, as Davenport the cook put a soya sausage in my mess tin with his fingers and slapped a small portion of dehydrated spud in on top of it.

'It's the last you'll get for a long time,' Davenport said, 'so think yourself lucky, sarge. We'll all be on hard tack from now on.'

'All except you, you fat sod,' Jones said with a laugh.

'Where's the char?' I said, holding out my other half of the mess tin.

'I've only one pair of hands,' Davenport remarked, 'so just help yourself.'

The tea always seemed to taste of burnt wood, and it was horrible. Yet it was warm, and helped down the dry sausage and spud, otherwise we would have gagged on it.

I was destined to get only half of my breakfast, for, as I walked away with Jones to find a spot to sit, I didn't take the usual precautions, and a 'shite' hawk pounced, nearly knocking my tin out of my hand. Its huge tallons closed on my breakfast.

'I'll just kill you, you thieving bastard,' I shouted as it flew off with a portion of my grub.

131

'I should have known better,' I said to Jones as we sat down under a tree.

'Those hawks will eat anything,' Jones said with a laugh. 'Even this muck.'

A few hours later, we were on the move, to seek out the Japs and attack, somewhere around the Mayu range, to join up with other troops of the 7th Indian Division; through jungle and swamps and malaria-ridden territory, knowing there was no turning back, but to stand and fight against the most fanatical foe known to man. Just to go through this jungle was enough to test any man. It was only fit for the wildlife that lived here. We got plenty of casualties from malaria and heat stroke and God knows what else. I wondered at times how I kept going as I moved around my platoon giving encouragement to the men under me.

I could feel those blood-sucking leeches on my sweaty body, and these could only be removed when we rested, and they caused ulcers so bad that you were left marked for life.

A few days later, we were in a consolidated position somewhere near Sinzweya in the Arakan. I had thought that C.S.M. Bell had malaria, and that had caused him to be like he was, but I was soon to learn the worst. He had just been round the company position with an officer when it happened, so suddenly that it took the officer by surprise. Bell just ran forward, past our position, yelling,

'Fight, you bastards!'

'Come back, you bloody fool, come back,' the officer called out, but Bell paid not the slightest heed. He kept on shouting and raving like a lunatic. The officer, realizing something was wrong, ordered two or three soldiers to get him and bring him back.

'You and you,' he said to two of the men, 'follow me.' And he ran towards Bell.

I saw them pounce on him, trying to hold him down.

'God Almighty. What's wrong with him?' I said aloud.

It took the officer and the two men all their time to keep a hold on him as they dragged him back. I daren't leave my position to help, but I saw his face as they passed. He was frothing at the mouth and still kicking and fighting with the men who held him. I stared at him until he was out of sight. It was a very disturbing and pathetic thing, to watch my friend, C.S.M. Bell affectionately known to his friends as Ding-Dong, being dragged away like that, and I knew that something was seriously wrong. But I had to dismiss my feelings for my friend as more sinister things confronted me and my unit out there in the jungle.

The 5th Division were attacking the Japs in the area. We were waiting for our artillery and tanks before we too went forward into the valley. Taung Bazar lay behind us and part of our troops were across the other side of the Kalapanzin river, while we were in the foot hills below the Mayu Ranges. After a couple of days, the order came to advance. Under our artillery barrage and meeting only small forces of Jap troops, and snipers high up in the trees that took a steady toll of our men, we moved forward until our objective was reached, where we consolidated our position, and were ordered to dig in.

Unknown to us at the time and to our Commanders, this move was a cleverly conceived plan. The Japs had lured us into a trap, as they thought, to destroy the 7th Indian Division. In simple terms, we were just like sheep being led to the slaughter. From here on, it was a fight for survival, against the most efficient and cunning jungle fighter the world has known. In my opinion, to fight a Jap was like fighting a demon, who went full out to destroy you and himself in the process.

Thank God we had a good and clever General, who not only evaded capture when his H.Q. were overrun, but, knowing what the Japs were up to, quickly appeared amongst us and organized our defence. That was to be known as the Admin Box. (Our offensive had become defensive.)

With our supplies, food and ammunition destroyed by the enemy in their first move, we found ourselves in a desperate position, and it was firmly believed by other Commanders in the Corps that we, the 7th Division, had been destroyed. With our supply dumps gone, it did seem hopeless.

The big Japanese offensive had begun. This was called the HA—GO offensive, hell bent on destroying the troops in Burma and moving into India. We, the 7th, were to be the first to go, according to the enemy. But they forgot one thing. That was the tenacity of the British troops when it came to a showdown like this. Of course, I praised the Jap as a jungle fighter. He was the greatest at hiding himself and sniping at you, or pretending to be dead as you advanced past him, then he would shoot you in the back, and he would fire at you from carefully concealed foxholes. But after all this time in Burma, we had learned his tricks and we, instead of being hunted, became the hunters. Later on in the campaign, this attack on the 7th Division was to become his first lesson in man-to-man fighting, and we were to turn this near-defeat into a great victory.

My platoon was dug in in slit trenches that just held two men, but in the fighting that ensued, these trenches were to become their graves. My job, like my officer's, was to move around all the platoon, and as the first attack came at dawn, I found I was in a trench with Mac, an Irish lad. Nobby my corporal and Len were in the next one quite nearby.

'Here they come, sarge,' Mac said in a whispered Irish brogue.

'I see 'em, Mac,' I replied, 'Are yer scared?'

'What do you think, sarge? Be Jesus I'm scared,' Mac said as he made the sign of the cross.

I did the same as I said, 'So am I, Mac, so am I.'

It was chilly and misty at this hour as the Japs moved slowly uphill, getting nearer and nearer, yet I was sweating profusely. I wiped my eyes with the back of my hand and looked at Mac.

'Not yet, Mac, wait until they are much nearer before you fire.'

I felt sick as I said it. I shit myself. I was shaking with fear and my mouth was so dry. My finger tightened on the trigger, waiting for the order to fire from our officer. I thought he was never going to shout.

'How close does he bloody want them to be?' I thought.

When all of a sudden it came—'FIRE!'. Hell was let loose as we opened up and Very lights shot into the sky, giving full light to the area and making the Japs good targets. They began to fall like skittles, yet more took their place.

I wasn't scared any more as I kept firing and hearing my officer shout 'Kill! Kill!' The shouting and screaming from the Japs made it worse, but I kept firing. I don't know why, but I was enjoying it.

'Don't let me down,' I said to my Sten gun, as I quickly changed magazines. I swung round quickly as I heard the Jap battle-cry. They had broken through to our rear. I fired up at the Jap officer who stood over our trench, swinging his sword. But it was too late for Mac. As I fired, I was covered in blood from Mac—his head left his body and the Jap, riddled with bullets, fell on top of me. I pushed his body over and jumped out of my trench, firing wherever the Japs appeared. I didn't intend that slit trench to be my grave.

The last thing I remember was a Jap rushing me, screaming as he lunged with his bayonet. I turned sideways as he thrust it at me. I felt a thud as it entered my backside, but before he could withdraw it, he too, fell lifeless. That shot came from Len. I fainted before I could say thanks.

I came to on an improvised stretcher, where the wounded were being attended to.

'God, it's hot,' I said to the medical orderly as he was dressing my wound. 'What's happened? Where's the Japs?'

'We beat them off, sarge, killing most of them,' the orderly replied. 'We showed them, didn't we?'

'Thank God,' I uttered. 'I thought it was our last. How bad is my wound?'

'It's but a flesh wound in the cheek of your bottom. It needed stitching, but you'll live,' the orderly said with a laugh. 'A couple of days and you'll be as good as new. I'm afraid you can't be sent back to hospital, it's not bad enough.'

'Have you heard how C.S.M. Bell is?' I asked.

'I'm afraid he's had it,' the orderly replied.

'What the hell do you mean, he's had it?' I said, sitting up. 'Where is he?'

'He's dead, sarge.'

'What? How?'

'He had rabies and he died horribly. I was with him. We had to tie him down. I have never seen anyone die of rabies before, and I never want to see another.'

I was so shocked, I just lay back without answering him. I covered my eyes with my hand. I didn't want the orderly to see me crying, for that's what I did. For my very close friend to die like that; for a man like him—it was unthinkable. Better to die fighting, than to go like a mad dog.

Our supplies were being dropped by the R.A.F., as the days went by slowly, and we repulsed all attacks from the Japs. We even heard 'Tokyo Rose' on our radios, telling us to surrender or die, as we were completely surrounded by thousands of Japanese Imperial Troops.

As night fell, and darkness enveloped us, we could hear the Japs out there calling, 'Help me, Johnny, it's me, help me'— pretending to be a British soldier wounded and helpless. Just another of the Japs' rotten tricks that we didn't fall for, yet it was still nerve-racking.

The swines had got through our lines all right, and they certainly surrounded us. We heard that our hospital had been attacked. The doctors, the nurses and the patients had been slaughtered, every single one of them. What kind of people were we fighting that would do a thing like that? I am quite sure that no other enemy but the Japs would slaughter the innocents, deliberately. They had no respect for life, not even their own. To beat this fox, we would have to kill every one of them, and believe me, that was our intention.

Our morale had always been poor in this filthy jungle, but not any more. These wicked beings made us into what we now were—killers. We knew the Chindits were harassing the Japs behind their lines, cutting off their supply routes, so that they had to depend on supplies that they could capture from us. This had been too easy for them before, now we weren't going to let them have anything of ours.

While we were pinned down here, the big Jap offensive was heading for Kohima and Imphal, the gateway to India. This was called the U-GO offensive. It was during a lull in the fighting when I again got out that little stub of pencil I carried and scribbled out another ditty:

> At Kohima, Imphal and the Arakan,
> Stood the British soldier, every man.
> The English, Irish, Scots and Welshmen too,
> With Indian and Gurkha, their forces grew.
> To meet the foe, in head-on clash,
> Midst roar of gun and bayonet flash.
> The blood is mingled with our sweat.
> 'Come, you bastards, we ain't through yet.
> We've a score to settle for our men who fell,
> And we won't stop now till you're all in Hell.'

Writing these ditties seemed to give me encouragement and got things off my chest. Each one I wrote, I put in my top left-hand pocket with the letters I had received from Kathleen, many months before.

Our defence of the Admin Box lasted around one month and,

with the help of reinforcements, we eventually beat off the Jap attack, possibly his first defeat in Burma. I must admit we were relieved to see this happen—to turn near-defeat into victory was without doubt, a great achievement, with the Japanese suffering great losses; at the same time, we lost around three to four thousand men.

I had remembered my father's words that he quoted—Nil Desperandum—never despair!

At long last we had become the hunters and the Japanese were routed. I had unashamed appreciation for the R.A.F. who kept us supplied, and the fighter-bombers who made this victory possible. I fell on my knees and prayed as the last remnants of Japs withdrew. We were weary, tired and filthy with lice, but we advanced like men reborn, capturing key positions that the Japs had taken when they started the HA-GO offensive.

The hospital where our people had been slaughtered was a shocking sight to see. All that was left, was their skeletons—the jackals and other wild animals had feasted on them.

I have never seen so many dead Japs as we moved forward, never. Lying in grotesque positions and covered with flies and ants—some were mere skeletons. I was glad to see them dead. The more dead, the better. For a God-fearing man, it was wrong to have these thoughts. You just had to be here to know the reason why. I would, and I knew it then, always hate the sight of a Jap soldier. We couldn't show them mercy as they never showed us any. We just had to exterminate them like one would a disease—it was the only way to victory.

While we advanced, fighting for every yard of jungle, big battles had started at Imphal and Kohima. Here, the Japs were attacking ferociously. The Jap held us in contempt. Why shouldn't he? We had run before and it was easy for them to advance—no wonder they held us in contempt. It was different now; we didn't run any more, but stood and fought. The same story was to unfold at Kohima and Imphal as it had here in the

Arakan. Without going into technicalities, I can only say in my own way that the offensive by the Japs was brought to a halt, and turned into an offensive by the British, but at great cost. Many thousands of British lives were lost in all these campaigns, but the losses to the Japs were tenfold.

At long last they were on the run, a thing we thought they weren't capable of doing. As I said before, I have never seen so many dead Japs at any one time. Some had even died of hunger and the wounded had fallen into puddles of mud and drowned, for during the campaign we encountered many a violent storm that turned places into quagmires.

Thousands also died of diseases which took British lives as well, but not in the same quantity. At times, I got twinges of remorse. The sight of these once victorious Jap soldiers was horrible and sickening and to overcome this remorse, I just thought of our own lads who had died so horribly at their hands. It was so hard to dislodge the Japs with their 'kamikaze' spirit. Just one, well-concealed bunker, with a half dozen Japs in it, could hold a thousand of our advancing troops up for quite a long time. They had to be dealt with individually.

It was doing just this that cost the life of my pal Len, and only a short time before my unit was pulled out for good and its place taken by fresh troops.

Poor Len, he would never see that little boy of his. As he lay dying in my arms, he asked me to get out the photo in his tunic pocket, but before he saw it he was dead. I stared at him for a few moments and then at the photo. It was Len's wife and his little boy. Written across the front were the words, 'To Daddy, with love' and signed.

'I'm sorry, Len, I'm bloody sorry. I can't help you as you helped me. It's too damn late.'

I looked up as the lads with flame-throwers were burning those rats alive in their foxhole.

'Goodbye, Len,' I said.

I had to move on. I knew the stretcher-bearers would pick

Len up. He would get a burial and not be left to the jackals.

A week or so later, my unit was replaced by fresh troops and we were withdrawn to India to a rest centre, where delousing, baths and cooked food were the order of the day.

I was promoted to C.S.M. but on my medical examination, I was down-graded. It was nothing serious, but it meant that if something unforeseen happened in the drive through Burma, and the unit had to return there, I wouldn't have to go. In fact, I was given a staff job in Calcutta for the last few months before the final surrender of the Japanese.

My close friends were dead, all except Sergeant Jones, Taffy and Nobby. We had a farewell drink together before I left. Gone were Bell, Len, Jock and Mac, and to me there would always be spaces in the ranks where these soldiers once stood.

Through Hell and back—that's where every soldier went in the Burma Campaign. Only those who were there knew this. Some never came back, they had only a one-way ticket.

Chapter Twelve

THE INTERLUDE

My stay here in Calcutta was quite the opposite. It went from the ridiculous to the sublime—I was in a good bed with sheets and had an Indian boy to look after me.

I left the war behind me, but somehow, it never left me. In the daytime, it was fabulous and the evenings off duty were unbelievable—the cafés that served exotic foods, the air-conditioned cinema and clubs, and the beautiful women of all nationalities. Knowing the war was nearly over, I settled down to enjoy the few months I had in my new job. But no matter what the days and evenings brought in enjoyment, at night as I lay in bed it all came back to me. I would toss and turn and wake up shouting and sweating profusely. I could see those slant-eyed men poking at me with their bayonets. I saw Mac's head fall in my lap. I threw it away in panic at its ghastly sight. I saw my friend Bell being lashed to a tree as he frothed at the mouth, and as I was cutting him free he tried to bite me.

'It's me, Spud,' I shouted at him, but it made no difference. He still snapped at me. I had to leave him tied up.

It was a nightmare, I knew, but what frightened me most was, whether they would persist, would these dreams affect me every night? God, I hoped not!

My job, together with an officer, was to provide entertainment for the men coming out of Burma. It was a job I enjoyed immensely, and it took my mind off those bad nights I was having.

I became quite professional at producing shows, both on

stage and on the radio. I came in contact with some famous people, like Jack Hawkins, the film star; he was a Major in charge of E.N.S.A. There was also his counterpart for the Americans, Melvin Douglas, and that great American singer, Tony Martin. Local talent amongst the Anglo-Indians was in abundance and they did so much for the troops, free of charge. People like Garny Niss and his Hawaian Band, Blossom Michael, the singer with his band, the Anderson Sisters, six of them; and many artistes from E.N.S.A. gave their services to me when they weren't doing their own shows. All great artistes, not what you'd call famous, but very professional. People like Harry Rawson from Liverpool, Ted Slater and Pat Gaye.

But one sticks out in my mind above all others, an Anglo-Indian lady known on All-India Radio as Queenie Wood, the pocket soprano. Her voice was just marvellous and the lads went mad about her.

I first heard her in church, singing *Ave Maria*. I knew I had to have her in my show, but would she come? That was the question. I waited until the service was over and confronted her as she left the church with her husband.

'Excuse me,' I said, as I stood in front of them. 'May I speak to you please?'

'Certainly,' she replied, with a smile. 'What can I do for you? I am in a hurry, I have another appointment.'

I thought at that moment that it was a brush-off, but I was wrong.

'I want you to sing in my show,' I said, rather nervously. 'I am Sergeant-Major——', but before I got my name out, she said, still smiling,

'Are you free at the moment?'

'I am,' I replied.

'Well, tell me on the way. Come with us.'

The Sikh driver held the door of his taxi open as we got in. 'Salaam, mem-sahib,' he said.

'It's very kind of you both to invite me along,' I said. I held out my hand as I introduced myself.

'My name is Queenie Woods and this is my husband, Cyril,' she said.

That meeting with this charming woman and her husband was the start of a very strong friendship, and it was through her that I wrote a letter to Kathleen, something that I hadn't done for a very long time.

When we reached our destination, I was invited in. It was an officer's club and I was their guest. Afterwards, they invited me to their home for dinner, or I should say, their city flat, for their proper home was a few miles out of the city.

As we entered the flat, we were greeted with respect by an Indian servant. I couldn't help but notice the large table so beautifully set ready for dinner. I also noticed that it was set for about eight people. The room itself was spacious and well furnished. A large electric fan hung from the ceiling, giving the room a cool atmosphere, and in the far corner was a grand piano.

'Please make yourself at home,' Queenie said. 'See to the drinks please, Cyril, won't you? While I get washed and changed. I won't be very long.'

'Thank you,' I said as I sat on the settee.

'Whisky and soda?' Cyril asked. 'What's your first name Sergeant-Major? We can't keep calling you Sergeant-Major.' He began to pour out two large whisky-and-sodas.

'My name? Oh, yes, it's Joe,' I replied.

'Good. Please call me Cyril and my wife Queenie. Everyone knows her by that name, all over India. Her real name is Orotund Regina DeCunha.'

'That's a lovely name. I have never heard the name Orotund before,' I said.

'That, I'm afraid, was given to her when her parents knew she could sing,' Cyril replied. 'It means clear and musical. There you are,' he said as he handed me a large drink. 'Good health.'

'Thank you,' I said 'All the best.'

We had been chatting and drinking for about twenty minutes, when Queenie walked into the room, looking so nice and fresh. Cyril and I stood up as she approached us. I wobbled a little.

'Oops, sorry,' I said.

'Sit down, both of you,' Queenie said, and she made herself comfortable in the armchair opposite.

'Now, tell me all about yourself.'

'I'll get you a drink,' Cyril said, getting up from the settee.

'Only a small tonic, please Cyril,' Queenie said. 'You were saying,' she went on.

'His name is Joe,' Cyril called out.

'Right, Joe, I'm listening.'

She just sat there, looking at me as I rambled on. I found her so easy to talk to. She never interrupted me, but just listened, and with the drinks I had consumed, I could talk.

'Lovely,' she said when I had finished. 'Now, I'm sure you must be hungry.' She looked at her wristwatch. 'Dinner will be ready in about fifteen minutes. Would you like to wash?'

'Yes, please,' I said.

'Cyril, stop drinking and show Joe the bathroom, please. He starts to drink and doesn't know when to stop,' Queenie said. 'Cyril, the bathroom please.' Queenie glared at him.

'Come on, Joe,' Cyril said, 'let's go.'

I felt better after the wash and much more sober. As I came out of the bathroom, I got rather a surprise. People were sitting at the table.

'This is Joe,' Queenie said to them. 'Joe, this is my mother, my sister Bobby and her husband Bob.'

'Pleased to meet you,' I said.

'Please sit there,' Queenie said to me, pointing to a chair.

'Khana tiayar haea,' the Indian servant said, meaning dinner is served.

'Shukria, Abdul,' Queenie replied ('Thank you, Abdul').

Cyril came to the table, quite unconcerned at being late. I

know we had a first course, I don't remember what it was; but I do know the curried chicken and rice was good. Only an Indian can make it like that. We finished with mango, an exotic Indian fruit.

'That was absolutely wonderful,' I said, as I dipped my fingers in my finger bowl and wiped them on my napkin. 'Just wonderful. I don't think I can move now, I am so full.'

'You enjoyed it, then?' Queenie asked.

'Enjoyed it? It was just great. I hope you don't think I'm rude, but one thing has been puzzling me.' Everyone at the table looked in my direction.

'What is that?' Queenie asked.

'Well, I have noticed that there are two more places set for dinner, as if you were expecting someone,' I said.

'Not really,' Queenie replied. 'It's just habit with us now. Quite often we do invite people, just like today, we invited you quite unexpectedly, and we know everything is ready.'

'I see, Very nice.' I really felt at home there, they were all so very friendly.

'Are you free tonight, Queenie?' her sister Bobby asked.

'Entirely free,' she replied. 'So we can sit back and relax. I am sure Joe has so much to tell us.'

'Yes, there is, but on one condition.'

'What is that?' Bobby asked.

'That you don't ask about Burma and the war That, thank God, is behind me and I don't want to be reminded of it. I hope you will excuse me for saying that, I don't want to offend you.'

'I quite agree with you, Joe,' Cyril said, 'and I'm sure we all understand, don't we?' he said as he looked at them all.

'Of course,' Queenie replied and the others nodded in agreement. 'Come,' she said. 'Let's make ourselves comfortable in the lounge.'

As we got up from the table, I said to Queenie, 'I know it is your night off, and I'm sure you are fed up with singing, and I don't like to ask you, but I must.'

Queenie stopped and put her hand on my arm.

'You want me to sing for you?' she asked.

'Well——'

She interrupted me and said,

'It will give me great pleasure to sing for you in just a little while.'

'Thank you so very much. I shall look forward to that.'

After we sat down and Cyril did the honours of serving the drinks, I started talking about my home and my family and Kathleen. They were very interested and very good listeners. But it was Queenie who said:

'Your girl, Kathleen. Tell me—you say she stopped writing to you quite a while ago?'

'Yes,' I replied.

'Well, did you ever stop to think that her letters might have got lost or your letters to her the same?'

'Not really,' I said. 'I just thought she might have got someone else and forgotten all about me. It hurt me for a while, and being where I was, I began to feel I might never get out of it, so I thought it was for the best.'

'Well, from what you have told me, I am sure she loves you,' Queenie said. 'Do you still love her?'

'More than anything,' I said. 'I think I always will. I sometimes wish I had never met her, you know, it would have been much easier for me.'

'Why, how's that?'

'Because when I go with any other woman now, or I'm just in their company, I see her face. I said to you not to mention Burma, but I must tell you this. I've never mentioned it to anyone before. You might laugh, but it's the gospel truth!'

'No, we won't,' Queenie said. 'Go on.'

'It's just that when I was at my lowest ebb, I wanted to give up. Do you know what I mean?' I said.

'I understand,' Queenie said, with a sort of worried look on her face. 'Please go on.'

146

There was a silence for a moment or two as I took a drink. I knew it was making me talk.

'It was then I used to see her face, Kathleen's, that is; she was there smiling at me. I seemed to hear her say "Joe"—then disappear. I wondered at times whether she was dead. You know, with the bombing and all that in England.'

I took another drink. They all seemed to be staring at me.

'I know you think it's daft,' I said, breaking the silence. I really felt a tear roll down my cheek (that's what a drop of whisky does). But when I looked at them, there was Queenie and her mother wiping their eyes. Queenie was the first to speak.

'It isn't daft at all, I think it is really sad.' And they all agreed. 'Now, Joe, you are going to make me a promise,' Queenie said. 'You want me to sing in your concert, do you?'

'Yes,' I said.

'That I'll do on one condition. I will only sing if you promise me, right now, that tomorrow, you will write a letter to Kathleen. I mean it,' she said.

'Cross my heart,' I said, putting my hand on my chest.

'Good,' Queenie said. 'I will sing for you.' And she stood up. As she walked to the piano, I was in for another surprise. She sat down and started to play, and she was as good a pianist as she was a singer. Her first song? Something unusual for her— *I'll take you home again, Kathleen*. I just sat back and listened and closed my eyes.

And that was how I came to write to my Kathleen again, after an interval of about twelve months or so.

Queenie went on to sing songs from her repertoire, such as *Vilia, O Vilia, Ave Maria, One Fine Day* from *Madame Butterfly*, and many more. I could have listened to her for ever. Her voice would have graced any opera house in the world. I was sorry when I had to say 'Goodnight'. But they took to me like I to them, and my visits to them became very frequent. Queenie sang in my show, as promised, because I had written a letter to

Kathleen, to which I was awaiting a reply.

During my term in this staff job in Calcutta, many a soldier stayed at the centre en route to Blighty and home, and quite a few passed through my hands, and plenty I knew so well. It was just great for me and them, to be able to give them as much comfort as I possibly could after knowing the conditions they had been through in Burma. But a lot of faces so familiar I never saw and never would—the lads left behind who gave their lives. I would have given my right arm to have seen Bell, Len, Mac, Jock and Billings and Lieutenant Fox. My God, wouldn't I!

After about three weeks from posting my letter to Kathleen, I received a reply. I knew it was from her before I opened it, by her handwriting. I would know it anywhere. My hand was shaking as I opened it. At least I knew she was safe, but what was I to learn from its contents! Was she married? It was open now, but my hand shook worse as I withdrew the neatly folded letter and began to read it.

My Darling Joe,
    Thank God you are safe and well. I have prayed for you every night before I went to sleep.
    When your letters stopped, I didn't know what to think. I just cried. Mama would say 'There will be a letter to-morrow', but tomorrow never came. My heart would give a jump when I heard the letter box rattle, only to be broken when it wasn't your letter.
    Now tomorrow has come at last. I got your letter. I am so glad I waited for you and I will marry you.

When I read this last paragraph, I just threw the letter in the air and shouted out loud with sheer joy. I couldn't contain myself. I must tell somebody, but who? I was alone in my room, so I just lay back on my bed and finished that lovely letter, from the only girl that ever really mattered to me. I read the letter over and over again until I knew it off by heart.

My stay in Calcutta was most enjoyable, to say the least, made possible with the civilian friends I had made, such as Queenie and her husband Cyril. The concerts that I organized and the parties that I went to gave me a taste of life at the top. I could have become part of that life, if I had taken the option of staying in India, for I was offered jobs by very influential people, and believe me, I was tempted.

Queenie and Cyril's home became my home. I wanted for nothing except one thing. The letter I had received from Kathleen decided me on that issue—the one thing above all this was Kathleen. I knew I must go home. I never doubted this for one single moment, even though I was many a time in the company of beautiful women, and in this magical Eastern atmosphere, to kiss their lips was fatal inasmuch as it sent your senses reeling, and they could quite easily make you forget about home.

I can't explain too well, but my love for Kathleen prevailed, and the more times I found myself in these situations, the stronger the longing became. The little voice in my head would say 'Kathleen is waiting for you'. So strong was this voice to me, that sometimes, I would leave a function and make my way home to my little room, where my Indian boy, who slept on the verandah would greet me. He would waken if a snake passed ten yards away, he was so faithful. Queenie and Cyril would be so worried if I left early, that one or other of them would 'phone the next day to see what was wrong.

I must have written every night I could to Kathleen, and it seemed as if from the time I left her to the time I had started to write again, the 'in between' had just been a bad dream.

Days, weeks and months went by and the day of repatriation got nearer, now that Japan had at last surrendered. Troops who had fought in the Burma campaign, were moving through on their way home. As new troops of occupation took their place, I knew then that it wouldn't be long before I was going too. I knew it would be hard for me to leave my friends, but that overwhelming desire to get home prevailed.

My friendship with Queenie and Cyril had grown strong. I liked Cyril a great deal, but I was deeply infatuated with his wife. Her voice, personality and generosity I let rule me, and unknown to me and through my stupid attention I gave her, she had fallen in love with me. I know it was all my fault, and when it came to light I could have kicked myself, for I wouldn't have hurt these two friends of mine for anything.

The first indication I got of this whole rotten business, was the night I went to dinner and found that Cyril had gone away on some pretence or other. Just Queenie, her sister and her husband, and her mother sat down to dinner. You could have cut the atmosphere with a knife. No one seemed very hungry, except Bobby's husband Bob. He seemed to be the only one really enjoying his food. Even Abdul was very quiet as he served the food. He usually had something to say. Something was wrong, I thought, but what? I felt uncomfortable, to say the least.

'May I get a drink, Queenie, please?' I asked.

'Help yourself,' she replied.

'Thank you and please excuse me,' I said as I got up from the table and went into the lounge where I poured out a glass of whisky and ginger. I drank it at once and then helped myself to another large one and took it over to the settee, where I sat down. I played with the glass in my hand, making no attempt to drink it. Queenie came over and sat near me.

'What's wrong with everyone tonight?' I said to her. 'Is it because Cyril's away?'

'Not really, dear,' she said, patting my knee. 'We will have a talk as soon as they have finished dinner.'

'Good,' I said. 'The suspense is killing me. I would like to know what is wrong with everyone.'

After they had all finished dinner and sat down, I tried to start a conversation, but Bobby seemed to be evasive and I knew we were getting nowhere.

So I stood up and said, 'I'll be going. I am up early to-morrow on duty. I'll give you a ring, Queenie.'

That did the trick.

'No, don't go Joe,' Queenie said. 'Please stay.'

'Why shouldn't he go?' Bobby asked. 'It is late.'

I looked at Bobby and I didn't like her expression one bit.

'I told you, Bobby, before, it has nothing to do with you. Please don't interfere in my affairs,' Queenie said. I stood there flabbergasted.

'Will someone please tell me what all this is about? It is absolutely stupid and if you don't come straight out with what you have on your mind, I'm off and I mean that.'

'I will tell you, Joe,' Bobby said, with a worried look on her face. 'I think it is my business, Queenie, so please excuse me.'

'Well Bobby, out with it,' I said.

Bobby looked at me for a moment or two before she spoke.

'Queenie thinks she is in love with you,' she said. 'She has told Cyril and he has gone to the villa. He's heartbroken. Please tell her, Joe, she is wrong to do this and that you are leaving India.'

I looked at Queenie.

'Is this right, Queenie? Did you tell Cyril this?'

'I have and I don't deny it,' she replied. 'I can't help how I feel, can I?'

'Maybe not, Queenie, but you have placed me in a peculiar situation, make no mistake,' I said. 'The way Bobby is talking, you would think I was to blame. You do, don't you, Bobby?'

'Do what?' Bobby asked.

'Blame me,' I said.

'I don't really know who to blame,' Bobby said. 'All I know is that it is stupid for Queenie to get like this. She has always been happy with Cyril, until you entered their lives, and now this.'

Queenie sat there, not uttering a word. I looked at her and said:

'I would appreciate it if I could discuss this matter with you and Cyril and not your sister. I appreciate her feelings, and concern about you, but I think it only concerns you and Cyril and me. Don't you agree? Well, don't you, Queenie?' I asked, quite in anger when she didn't answer me. She could see I was angry.

'I will ring him tomorrow,' she said, 'and make some arrangement.'

'Do that by all means, and I won't come here until you contact me. Goodnight, all,' I said, as I went to the door. As I opened it, I looked back.

'Don't forget, Queenie, when you have spoken to Cyril and made some arrangement, contact me. Goodnight again,' I said, before I closed the door.

It was a dangerous thing for me to do, when I decided to walk home, to cool off really. That little confrontation had upset me. I would, as a rule, get a taxi, as it wasn't really safe to walk alone at night, and I was beginning to wish I had done so, as I hurried through the dark and narrow streets, nearly falling over sleeping Indians on the pavements, and being confronted with beggars asking for 'buckshees', to whom I tactfully gave something. What a fool I was, I thought, when I saw sinister figures lurking in darkened passages and doorways.

I felt for my knife that I always carried in a sheath strapped to my forearm. I turned quickly, drawing my knife, when I heard a noise. I started to sweat as I stood waiting for someone to pounce on me. Then I saw the culprits, scurrying amongst the garbage—rats, big, brown rats that infested the city at night. I wiped my forehead.

'Thank God,' I said out loud, and keeping my knife in my hand, I quickened my steps.

'Hey, ghari muntai,' I shouted as I saw an Indian squatting near his horse and ghari, smoking a 'beadi'.

'Kither jiaga, sahib?' he said, as he spat out a mouthful of betel nut, a horrible red substance.

'Chowringee jiaga, gilti,' I replied.

'Teeki, sahib', he said, as he got into the driving seat and started on his way. I heaved a sigh of relief as we turned from the narrow streets and into the welcome and well-lit main street that I knew. One couldn't trust the ghari wallahs if they knew you were on your own and thought you were easy pickings.

On arrival, I went straight to my quarters, undressed and had a shower. Then getting a bottle of whisky and some ginger ale that I placed on my locker, I sat on my bed, thinking and drinking. I was thinking what I could do over this new development with Queenie and Cyril.

I must have fallen asleep for it was well after midnight when my boy woke me. I heard knocking on the door.

'Sahib, sahib, are you awake? Mam-sahib here.'

I hurried to the door.

'What the hell is it, Ahmed?' I said angrily. 'Which mam-sahib?'

He just smiled as Queenie walked towards me.

'It's me Joe. I just had to see you, I just had to.'

'Well, come in before you are seen, for God's sake, otherwise I'll get shot.' I pulled Queenie by the arm, inside, and closed the door. 'What the hell are you doing out at this time, Queenie? You know it's dangerous,' I said.

'It's quite all right. Abdul brought me. I couldn't come to any harm, he would see to that,' Queenie replied.

'Just the same, how are you going to get back? I saw Abdul drive off.'

Queenie looked at me before answering.

'Well?' I said.

'I'm staying with you tonight.'

'But Queenie, you mustn't.'

She put her arms round my neck and drew me to her, giving me a long, passionate kiss. With the whisky I had drank and Queenie holding me so close as she kissed me, I lost all control. My arms found their way around her body and I squeezed her tightly.

'I love you so,' Queenie said, as I held her. 'I can't help it.'

'I love you, Queenie darling, but not in the way that you want me to. So please don't hurt yourself any more You know I love Kathleen and I intend to marry her when I go home. Nothing and nobody will stop me from doing that, Queenie, and you above anyone should know that. Please think of her. What would she say if she thought I was with you, and me asking her to marry me? And think of Cyril—what has he done to deserve this? Bobby was right tonight when she said that you and Cyril were all right before I came. Now I feel so damn guilty, but I also feel flattered by your love. I do honestly.'

Queenie was silent as she rested her head on my shoulder. She looked up at me.

'You think I am cheap, don't you? You don't know how I feel, what it is doing to me inside. God only knows my torment. I have grown to love you. I know it isn't fair to Cyril, to my family or to that beautiful girl of yours, Kathleen. Don't you think I have thought of this? Do you think I am made of iron? My God,' she said as she pulled away from me and sat down. She was crying. She talked between sobs, telling me I could have anything, that I would want for nothing. I let her talk, as I filled my glass with whisky, and drank.

'It's no good, Queenie, carrying on like this, and you know it. Please just let us be friends and leave it at that. My mind is fully made up. I am going home and you must go back to Cyril before it is too late, to make amends. You will realize it's for the best, and maybe one day, you will thank me for being, as you think, so cruel,' I said. 'Come on, dry your eyes, love. Here's a drink for you.'

Queenie took the drink that I offered her.

'Go on, drink it,' I said. 'It will buck you up.'

Afterwards, we just talked and talked.

'Queenie,' I said. 'Tonight's our night—you and I. It will be the beginning of the end of our affair. What do you say?'

Queenie seemed to resign herself to the situation. She looked at me with tear-filled eyes.

'I agree to that,' she said as she stood up and put her arms around me. 'Tonight is ours,' she said.

Six weeks later, I left Deulali, the reception centre I had loathed when I arrived in India; but now, it was paradise. From here, thank God, I was on my way home—on my twenty-fifth birthday—October 1945.

Chapter Thirteen

HOMEWARD BOUND

I was allotted a cabin coming home, with three more warrant officers. It was like a cruise, every day a holiday, a ship of happiness. Even those poor unfortunate ex-prisoners of the Japs that I used to see being brought up on deck from the ship's hospital to enjoy the sunshine and our company, were beginning to take pleasure in life.

I just couldn't help reflecting on that stinking war in Burma, where I saw these lads, just skin and bone. Some of these were doomed to die. I talked to some of them as they talked about seeing 'this green and pleasant land' that we had sung about so often.

I could visualize all the people in my town especially greeting me and my brothers, flags flying and bands playing.

'It will be just great,' I told them, and I firmly believed this myself. Hadn't the lads beaten the Germans in Europe and the Middle East? Hadn't we done the same with the Japs in Burma —even before we dropped the bomb on Japan? Of course we would all be welcomed home like heroes! It would all be different from when my Dad came home from the 1914 war. We would have houses to live in and jobs to go to—this we had been promised and I looked forward to it, like all the other chaps. Yes, this homeward-bound boat was a happy boat indeed.

One thing only marred my complete happiness—I could never shake off those nightmares that still persisted.

It took approximately five weeks for our ship to reach

Southampton. I think everyone was on deck from the time of the first sighting and all the soldiers on board were shaking each other's hands. Here, I got my first setback. I lost my war trophies. We had to declare them—things I wanted to keep were taken—my Japanese sword and revolver. Some were just lucky and got away with theirs.

Nevertheless, I was on my way home and wasn't I going to be married to the only girl who mattered, Kathleen, who had waited for me for so long? Blow the trophies, I thought.

From Southampton to London, then the night train to Manchester.

I couldn't sleep, neither could my companions on that train. We must have sung ourselves hoarse, until we arrived around five o'clock in the morning.

'Not a bloody soul around,' someone said as we stepped off that train so early in the morning. 'Except the railway staff.'

'Christ, what a reception,' someone else called out.

'Wakey, wakey!' he shouted. 'We're home.'

'Tickets please,' was the only response we got to that, as we went through the barrier.

'Cheerio, good luck.' This could be heard as everyone went their different ways and each one of us was in a hurry to get home.

What time did my train leave for the last stage home?, I wondered, as I looked at the time table. I saw it was at seven o' clock—two long hours to wait. Then, as a porter passed, I asked him.

'Ay, that's reet, it'll be at seven o'clock. Why doesn't tha ask if there's a van goin' your way? Tha knows, one of them paper vans, over theer,' he said, pointing to some vans, being loaded with newspapers.

'Thanks,' I said, as I slung my kitbag over my shoulder. 'I will.'

I hurried over to where the vans were.

'Anybody here going to——?'

'Ay, I am,' some chap called back.

'Can yer give me a lift?' I asked.

'I will that, lad. I'll be ready to leave in ten minutes. Jump in,' he said.

'Thanks a lot,' I said, as I threw my kitbag on the stack of newspapers in the back of his van, and got in.

'I don't know you, do I?' I said to the driver as he got in. 'Do you know me, I'm Joe Murphy?'

'No, I dunna,' he replied, 'I've only just moved up theer. I bowt this shop and I'm sort of a stranger yet. Weer does tha want dropping?'

'Near gasworks,' I replied. 'If that's O.K. with you.'

'Ay, that's fine. I pass theer,' he said.

I settled down in my seat as he drove off, and believe me, I talked him to death, as he sped through the lonely wet streets. It had started to rain.

'Are yer folks expecting yer?' the driver said.

'Well, I sent a telegram from the ship at Southampton,' I said, 'but they won't know what time I'll be arriving. But I don't care. All I know is that I'm nearly home. It's been a long time, a bloody long time.'

It was raining quite heavily now, but I didn't worry. I was so excited as we drew nearer and nearer. Then all of a sudden, he stopped.

'Here you are lad. This is your street,' the driver said.

'Yes, my friend, this is my street. Thanks for the lift.' I said, as I opened the door and got out into the pouring rain.

'Ay, don't forget this,' the man said, as he passed out my kitbag and said 'Good luck.'

I threw the large bag over my shoulder and watched him drive away. I just stood there, a lone figure, not worrying about the rain that beat down, as I looked up that old cobbled street, wet and dark, that old gas lamp on the corner giving it its only light, and just the noise from that pumping machine from the gasworks breaking the early morning silence.

'Don't just stand there lad, start walking. What did you expect to see? A brass band? Flags flying—and everyone waiting to greet you?'

That little voice in my head was talking again. Yes, I did want a band to greet me, I wanted all the bloody town to greet me. Why not? Haven't I been at war? I answered that voice in my head.

'Now you know how your Dad before you felt when he came home. He came home to nothing and you must do the same.' But it's not fair, it's not bloody fair, I shouted back as the tears mingled with the rain on my face. I started to walk towards the locked door of my home.

As I drew near, I looked up and saw a flag hanging from the bedroom window. Even that didn't flutter, it hung limp and wet. Just one solitary Union Jack from my family.

> 'No homage paid to you m'lad,
> Just your brothers and sisters, mam and dad.'

I remembered those words so well.

My house was in darkness, but they didn't know what time I would arrive home. They will know now, I said to myself, the whole street will know. Then I let out a yell:

'YIPEE! WAKEY, WAKEY! IT'S ME, MAM, JOE. I'M HOME!'

'It's our Joe, Mam,' I heard Tom shout. 'Where's those bloody matches?'

I saw the light go on in the bedroom, then in the downstairs room. The bolt on the door was pulled across and the door opened. I just dropped my kitbag as I saw my mam.

'Oh, Mam,' I said as I flung my arms round her and hugged her tight as she held me.

'Joe, love,' she said, as she began to cry. I saw Dad coming towards me. I held out one arm to greet him.

'Hello, Dad,' I said.

'Hello, son, you made it,' he said. 'Thank God,' then kissed me on my cheek. That man of iron who I had said had no emotion, kissed me on my cheek.

'It's grand to be home, Dad, just grand.'

'Come on, Lizzie,' Dad said to Mam, 'let the lad go, and get him some breakfast. I'm sure he's hungry.'

'A good idea, Mam,' I said. 'I could eat a horse, cart an' all.'

'Right, love,' Mam replied, as she took her arms from around my neck and kissed me again. 'A breakfast fit for a soldier.'

'Where's Hilda, Kathleen and Brian?' I asked Dad.

'The girls will be down in a minute. They go to work at eight o'clock. As for young Brian, the Army's sent him to India.'

'What?' I said. 'Young Brian gone to India? And me just leaving there. Surely he's not old enough to be in the army, is he? And the girls working too? I just can't believe it. That smells good, Mam,' I shouted as I got the smell of bacon coming from the kitchen.

'Wash yer hands, love,' Mam called back. 'It won't be long.'

I looked round the room. Nothing had changed one bit. Even the old black kettle was boiling on the hob, and up on that high mantelpiece were extra photos of my brothers and myself. Six of us, proudly displayed there in our uniforms, and Dad's, still prominent in the centre. I thought to myself how proud Mam and Dad must have been.

'Come on, Joe,' Mam said, as she put my breakfast on the table. 'Get yer hands washed and have this.'

'Right away, Mam,' I said, as I took off my tunic and hurried into the kitchen. The lead pipe on the wall was still loose. I started to sing to myself as I washed.

'That looks good, Mam,' I said, coming into the room wiping my hands on the towel. 'But there seems a lot. I hope you aren't doing without yourselves. We're still on ration.'

'Just sit down,' Dad said, 'and forget about the bloody rationing. Enjoy your breakfast. Good God, it'd be a poor show if we couldn't have bacon and eggs for thee coming home.'

'I'll enjoy it, Dad, I promise you,' I said, as I began to tuck in. I noticed that the table was covered with a nice white cloth, and thought how nice it looked. I remembered the days of yesteryear when that same old table was covered with newspapers to keep the scrubbed top clean, because then Mam didn't have a cloth to put on.

I was alone now at the table. As I looked round, I imagined Tom, John, Frank, Jim and Brian there. I stopped eating for a moment, just staring and remembering.

It would never be the same again. Nothing would be the same. Young Brian had been sent to India by the army, John, Frank, Jim, who were married, had returned to take up life with their own families down south.

Tom was here, but bad with bronchitis, and had to work at the gasworks. Curse the bloody war.

'What is it, love? Why don't you eat?' Mam said.

I looked at her before I replied.

'Nothing, Mam,' I said, as I began to eat my breakfast. 'I was just thinking, that's all, just thinking.'

After breakfast, I just sat and talked to Mam and Dad. Tom came downstairs just before Hilda and Kathleen. Poor Tom had been through a great deal and was in ill health—that's what the war did for him.

'Well, owd lad,' he said, when he saw me.

'Tom,' I said, jumping up off my chair. 'It's great to see you.'

'You too, Joe.' He grasped me firmly by the hand. 'I have to go to work now, so I'll see you tonight.'

'O.K., Tom,' I said, as he went to have a wash.

When Hilda and Kathleen came to the table, I got a surprise. They were young women.

'I wouldn't have known you two,' I said as I gave them a kiss. 'Those few years have made a difference.'

After Tom and the girls had gone to work, I busied myself getting my kit sorted out, having a bath; and I had to see Mrs. Bennett and our other neighbours to let them know I was home.

But at the forefront of my mind, above all else, was that I had to get over to Ireland as soon as I possibly could to see Kathleen. I had sent a telegram from the ship, telling Kathleen of my arrival in England. Now I must send another one, telling her I was going over there. This I did right after lunch. I wasn't to know of all the obstacles in my way of getting to Ireland, when I sent it off. Restrictions were in force, preventing me from going. It was to be two more long weeks and a dozen telegrams later, before I was to see Kathleen. I was at my wits' end with all the red tape, and during these two weeks I realized I wasn't the same man that I was before the war.

My nightmares persisted, most nights, although no one knew of them. I was irritable and impatient. I couldn't settle properly. I contented myself with the thought of getting married to Kathleen and setting up home together. I was sure things would be different when we were married. We would have a nice house, have a family, I would get a good job—of course things would be all right.

At long last, the day arrived. I was on my way. Kathleen was to meet me in Dublin. I was so excited, and so was my Mam, when I set off on this, my final journey to the girl who really mattered in my life, the girl who had waited for me all those years.

The train was waiting at the platform as I got off the boat—the train to Dublin and Kathleen, just six miles away.

I stood at the carriage window from the moment it left, and I never sat down once, as my excitement grew. It was the longest six miles of my whole life.

I had the door open as the train reached the platform. As I got out, I placed my case down and looked round for Kathleen. I just let all the other passengers pass me, until they had all gone, hidden by a cloud of steam from the train. My heart seemed to fall, I couldn't see her.

But as the steam cleared, I heard a voice.

'Joe! Joe!'

I looked and saw her at the barrier, waving.

'Kathleen,' I shouted at the top of my voice, 'Kathleen.'

I ran to meet her as she came towards me. With my case forgotten and my arms outstretched, we met and held each other in one long embrace.

'Oh, Kathleen, my Kathleen,' I whispered as I kissed her. 'It's been so long, so very, very long.'

We were oblivious to everyone as we embraced. I was, at last, with the girl I loved. Nothing else mattered.

I didn't have to look back any more with tears. For the tears in both our eyes were tears of joy and hope for our future together.